TOP SECRETS FOR SALES SUCCESS

101 SECRETS THAT SOLD $$$MILLIONS

Philip Belcher

SalesAbility

Copyright © Philip Belcher, SalesAbility 2019

This book is Copyright. All rights reserved. Other than any use permitted under the Copyright Act, no part of this book including information storage and retrieval systems, without permission in writing from the publisher, except by reviewers who may quote brief passages in a review.

ISBN 978-0-6487475-9-8   Paperback Edition
Catalogue in Publication Data
Philip Belcher
Top Secrets for Sales Success

Some characters in this book are fictitious. Any similarity to real persons, living or deceased, is coincidental and not intended by the author

Edited by: Julie Belcher
Front Cover Artwork: Philip Belcher
Book Design by: SalesAbility
Photography by: jazzyphotography.com.au
Printed and bound in Australia by: intertype.com.au
First printing: January, 2020

Published by: SalesAbility

Visit: www.salesability.com.au

DISCLAIMER AND/OR LEGAL NOTICES

Whilst the author and publisher have made every effort to ensure that the information in this book was accurate at the time of publication, the author and publisher hereby disclaim and do not assume any liability to any party for any loss, damage or disruption caused by errors or omissions, whether such errors or omissions result from negligence, accident or any other cause.

References to individuals are based on publicly available sources. Any aspersions or derogatory inferences are unintentional. This work is general and should not be deemed specific to the reader. Whilst these methods have been used by the author to good effect, no guarantee or warranty is either expressly or by inference offered as to the success of applying the methods contained in this book. The author and publishers are not psychologists so this book is general in nature and does not represent any professional behavioural, psychological or similar advice. Where the reader feels that they may have any personal issues they should immediately seek qualified professional advice.

Contents

Dedication 11

Welcome! 15

My Top Ten Secrets for Sales Success: 19

My Top Sales Secrets 22

Personal Development 23

   1. The Golden Rule: I treat others as I want to be treated ... 25

   2. I keep myself in good shape 26

   3. I look like someone my target customers would trust 27

   4. I know there is no straight line to success 28

   5. It is my duty to help my customers to address their needs .. 30

   6. My reputation is my greatest asset 31

   7. Making Target is to be celebrated 32

   8. I love being in sales because I address people's needs 34

   9. I look in the mirror to find out who is responsible 35

   10. I mentor others toward achieving their full potential 36

   11. Peers see me as a leader in sales excellence 38

12. I read, listen and watch every day to improve myself 39

13. My product knowledge is always beyond what I need 40

14. I am an excellent time manager 41

15. I can manage multiple tasks in parallel 43

16. I offer praise in abundance and criticism sparingly 44

17. I am an excellent presenter and public speaker 45

18. I seek the opportunity to speak in public regularly 46

19. I study the Masters in business and selling 48

20. I have outstanding mentors to assist me 49

21. I have a clear, current set of written goals that I review 50

22. I have a balanced life 51

23. I take time out to "Charge my Batteries" 52

24. I focus on doing more of what went well 54

25. I can relate current events to my customers' situation 55

26. True success doesn't demand applause 56

27. People seek me for advice and mentorship 57

28. I have many stories to tell that inspire 59

29. I don't waste time absorbing things that won't assist me ... 60

30. I study the Great People and learn from them................... 61

31. I am young at heart and strive to be wise........................... 62

32. I learn from those I consider to be more experienced 64

33. I admit my errors then work to correct them..................... 65

34. I have a verse that gets me through the darkest times 66

35. I know that I am NOT my title or my job 67

36. I am even-tempered 69

37. I have mentors that guide me toward success 70

38. I focus on the big things 71

39. I truly love my life as a successful salesperson 72

Technique 75

40. I have two eyes, two ears and one mouth.......................... 77

41. I ask questions, I don't tell 78

42. My customers are always happy to offer me referrals........ 79

43. I never call on my clients when it will annoy them 81

44. I only sell what I am passionate about.............................. 82

45. I know the trick is that there is no trick in selling 83

46. Customers buy for their reasons, not mine 85

47. I continually ask questions until I identify true needs........ 86

48. I don't jump to conclusions about the true needs 87

49. I know that customers buy with their emotions first 89

50. My Sales manager is my best ally at work 90

51. I am my toughest sales manager 91

52. My admin work is always completed on time. 93

53. I put in the work "up front" on a sales opportunity 94

54. I know that the best 'close' is the one that is never needed 95

55. I am second to none at closing sales 97

56. I focus on fulfilling my customers' needs.......................... 98

57. I never leave home without my business cards.................. 99

58. I have a 1 minute "Customer Value Pitch"......................100

59. No matter what my title, I am ALWAYS in Sales! 102

60. The millionaire next door looks like the rest of us 103

61. I know the WIIFM (What's In It For Me) 104

62. I understand the customer politics 105

63. I have done the work required to make the sale 107

64. I write thank you notes to my customers and prospects .. 108

65. I delight my customers 109

66. I am an expert in the eyes of my customers 110

67. I can explain how my offering is of financial benefit 112

Strategy 115

68. I am a student of strategy and use it to increase my sales. 117

69. My pipeline is the life blood of my income 118

70. I make my own game and don't compete in others 119

71. My existing customers are seven times easier to sell to ... 121

72. My company makes 80% of profit from 20% of products 122

73. 80% of my prospects will contribute 20% of my sales 123

74. 20% of my clients will provide 80% of my sales 124

75. I know Sales success is about focus 126

76. The customer relationship begins after the sale is closed. 127

77. I spend 50% of my time on customers that can buy 128

78. I know who the decision makers are for the sale 129

79. I know how to use the market conditions 131

80. My competitors are not aware of my strategies 132

81. I know who my competitors are and how to compete 133

82. I take advantage of events, no matter how small 134

83. My network is one of my greatest assets 136

84. I am a student of the economy 137

85. I look for advantage out of every adverse situation 138

Execution 141

86. If it needs done, I do it now! 143

87. I treat my colleagues and support team as customers 144

88. I plan my activities well in advance 145

89. I prioritise what I will do 147

90. I always arrive with time to spare 148

91. Sales is all about the numbers and I always know mine ... 149

92. I have a great support team that I constantly reward 151

93. I plan my next day before I finish for the day 152

94. The best days to visit customers are bad weather days 153

95. I spend 80% of my prospecting time qualifying 154

96. I use sales systems to their fullest and assist others 156

97. I take time out to think before I act, then act decisively .. 157

98. I diligently communicate with my customers 158

99. No one succeeded by getting 100% for doing nothing 160

100. I get the best facts available then act decisively 161

101. My plans are useless unless I put them into action 162

Last but not least 165

102. Closing Secret: ENJOY!! 167

Bibliography 169

Recommended Reading 170

Dedication

This book is dedicated to the people who, even though they may not know, or have known it, have inspired, supported and mentored me throughout my extensive career as a sales professional/leader. You will know who you are.

Especially:

Julie, my life long partner and 'rock' who has supported me through thick and thin as well as editing this book. Love you always!

Kate, Sarah, Jessica, James and your wonderful families; you continue to provide the inspiration that I built a career upon! Without you and your tireless patience and unwavering support, none of this would have happened.

Margaret who imparted her wisdom of "no matter what you choose to be, even a 'garbage collector', make sure that you are the very best that you can possibly be at it!" I'm still working on it, Mum… and always will!

Victor for showing me that if you can picture great things in your mind, then you can make them happen provided that you work hard, put in the necessary long hours and above all: never give up! Thanks Dad.

Vicki for being the big sister that set the example to strive for a higher level of learning when I was a kid and Graeme for being the big brother that I never had.

Last and so importantly, Kaye for being the inspiring 'nothing's too hard' person who has always been there for me and the family through thick and thin!

My sincere thanks to you one and all!

The will to win, the desire to succeed, the urge to reach your full potential... these are the keys that will unlock the door to personal excellence.

—CONFUCIOUS

Welcome!

You are reading this because you want to be a success in selling. Great! Just by purchasing this book, you have taken a major step in your quest for sales excellence.

Like everyone else, you want the 'Magic Secret' to sales success. OK, here it is.

If you are going to be a success in selling, you must live by 'PAWS':

Positive Attitude, strong Work ethic and always think/act Strategically.

You MUST be highly motivated, passionate and tirelessly work in a strategically focused method to be a success in selling!

But there is a 'speed bump'! No one can motivate you!!

Only you can motivate yourself!!

In all the hectic activity, endless demands and high level of stress in our daily sales lives, it is all too easy to forget to ensure that your ideas are focused on being the best salesperson you can be.

I have found that the secret to success is having a mental catalogue of inspiring ideas or 'hooks', similar to the catchy line in a song that you can't get out of your head, to secretly repeat to yourself at any time when needed to face sales challenges. Because these thoughts are private, with you keeping them to yourself as you go about your hectic activities, I call them 'Secrets'.

Having these Secrets at the front of your mind can make all the difference when the heat is on, akin to having a cool drink on a hot day.

Here is a selection of my Secret ideas that I have used in my career to personally make sales of <u>100s of Millions of dollars</u>' and manage my teams to sell $Billions worth of goods and services.

Whilst these Secret ideas are often well known or just plain 'common sense', once you are made aware of them, you can adopt them to use in your own unique way as *your* **Secrets for Success**.

These Secrets are what you regularly tell yourself but don't usually share with anyone else as you go about your mission on a day to day basis. You may be sitting in front of a customer dealing with their needs whilst secretly referring to these ideas to use them to advance the sale and win the business.

Used effectively, these ideas will become your *'secret weapon'* that will leave others wondering "How does she/he do it?"

The Secrets are arranged in no particular order in four hierarchical sections:

- **Personal Development**
- **Sales Technique**
- **Strategy**
- **Execution**

It is said that 'To become, you must be'. To become a highly successful salesperson requires one to be a person with the necessary attributes. Successful salespeople understand that they continually seek personal development.

Sales techniques can be learned and honed using the sales professionals' attributes that they continually hone.

As a well-prepared sales professional with the necessary attributes and sales techniques, a 'plan of approach' or strategy is required. The more refined the strategy, the greater likelihood of success.

Once a well thought out and researched strategy is developed, precise and continual execution of that strategy is mandatory for success. It is this area where many salespeople and their organisations fail. The road of failure is littered with wall charts and strategy documents developed in expensive 'Off-site Kick offs' and 'Strategy Retreats' that have never been executed or implemented. Everyone gets excited, enjoys the event and then goes back to 'doing things as they have always done them'. The highly successful salespeople know that relentless execution is the difference between them and others that wallow in mediocrity.

To get the most out of these secret ideas, scan them to find the ones that are most applicable to your current circumstances, write them down, read them before retiring for the night and then read them again in the morning before you start your day.

Pick the one(s) that you feel will 'get you over the hump' that you are facing and repeat them during the day. Remember the 'Power of 3'. Don't try to take on more than three secrets to inspire yourself at any one time. Your mind works best when it can focus. If just one 'secret idea' will make all the difference to the challenge you are facing, great: keep repeating it to get you through. Any more than three at a time will defuse the power of the secrets because your mind won't be clear on any one of them.

I don't promise that using these secrets will work, but there again, you are better off repeating them to yourself than listening to that other 'negative voice' in your head that keeps saying "It'll never work" or "They'll never buy that" or "I don't think I am cut out for this" or any number of other negative ideas that drain your energy and <u>will be true if you let them take over.</u>

MAKE SURE YOU WRITE ALL OVER THIS BOOK.

You paid good money for this book. *It's yours* so scribble to your heart's content! At the front of the book are pages for you to write down your own "Top 10 Secret Ideas of the Day".

There is a NOTES area at the end of every Secret for you to write your ideas and actions that you will take. If you like something that you hear, read or create yourself, write it in this book and then go back over it regularly.

Enjoy and vigorously apply these secrets. Above all else, enjoy your time in what is, in my opinion, one of the finest careers that you can undertake - Sales!

Good Selling!

My Top Ten Secrets for Sales Success:

[In no particular order, other than the Golden Rule which is **always** first!]

The Golden Rule ❧

I treat others as I want to be treated when I am a customer!

Top Sales Success Secret 1: ❧

Top Sales Success Secret 2. ❧

Top Sales Success Secret 3. ❧

Top Sales Success Secret 4. 🖎

Top Sales Success Secret 5. 🖎

Top Sales Success Secret 6. 🖎

Top Sales Success Secret 7. 🖎

Top Sales Success Secret 8. 🖎

Top Sales Success Secret 9. 🖎

Top Sales Success Secret 10. 🖎

NOTES

My Top Sales Secrets

-

-

-

-

Section 1

Personal Development

1. The Golden Rule: I treat others as I want to be treated when I am a customer!

If there is only one thing that you ALWAYS do as a result of buying this book, make it this one. Every time you have contact with a customer, think "if I were the customer, how would I want to be treated?" Get this right and you will be so much better than the vast majority of salespeople.

Every day we experience examples of salespeople breaking this rule. We take goods to a counter in a retail store and wait, only to have someone that arrived after we did get served before us because the sales clerk was not paying attention.

There are 'wait staff' in restaurants, who are in reality salespeople, that fail to pay attention and ignore us so that we have to call them for simple matters like asking for them to take our order or to get the bill. Imagine; you the customer needing to ask to pay them money?

Imagine going to buy a vehicle with your spouse. You and your spouse let the salesperson know that it is you that will make the decision to buy the car. Your spouse continually reminds the salesperson that it is you that will make the decision, yet they persist in overlooking you to talk with your spouse. The salesperson would not want to feel demeaned or treated as irrelevant so why do they treat you like that? I had this happen to my wife and me recently when we were buying a vehicle for her. I had to keep telling the car salesperson (actually sales-_man_) to talk with my wife because it was going to be her car. He just couldn't get it. Eventually he did and we bought the car but it took a lot of patience on the part of my wife – and me.

In every potential transaction ask yourself "How would I want to be treated in this situation?" and then go about providing sales service to your customers as if it was to you.

Doing this one thing alone will increase your sales volume and 're-peat business' massively because there are so few salespeople that do it. Remember the equation and apply it every day:

Applying the Golden Rule
= Delighted Customers
= Big $$$s of ongoing sales.

NOTES:

---

2. I keep myself in good shape

You cannot be successful in sales if you are struggling to keep up because you are unfit. You don't have to be a marathon runner (although that's not a bad idea) but regular exercise, healthy diet and a good night's sleep keeps you sharp and ready to sell.

Staying in shape must form part of your goals and then cascade into your time management.

Each of us has their own personal likes and dislikes when it comes to exercise. The act of making the decision to exercise and doing it is half the battle. Walking is a great method and can be done anywhere, anytime –even if it is raining or cold. If you are more energetic you can get some decent running shoes and jog/run or get into the gym. Of course, there are so many other forms such as bicycle riding, swimming, rowing etc.

Anything that you can do to get your heart rate up and breathing deeply on a regular basis will do you no end of physical and mental good. The blood moving through your body takes much needed oxygen to your vital organs and provides a welcome relief from the daily 'grind'.

An important benefit of exercise is that you are free to think. It is amazing how exercising gets you thinking and how often solutions and ideas 'pop into your mind' that you were not expecting.

The decision to exercise and then actually doing it is positive reinforcement that you are in control of your destiny. Make an appointment with yourself for the time to spend exercising and treat is as if it were a critical business meeting.

You would not 'bump' a meeting with an important client if you knew it would ruin your chances of being successful. Your fitness is an essential component in you having the stamina that is required to be a top performer so why would you 'bump' an appointment with yourself to stay in shape? Focusing your thinking and being creative whilst exercising can lead to 'break-through' ideas that could earn you a fortune. Missing out on your time for yourself exercising and that associated thinking is not an option.

"I keep myself in good shape" applies to your body – and to your mind.

NOTES:

3. I look like someone my target customers would trust

Sales is not a beauty contest however we all have a preconceived idea of what the person looks like that we would trust to provide an important service to us.

We wouldn't eat in a restaurant if the staff looked like road workers or let a doctor in a mechanics clothes operate on us. In the same way, we will not trust a salesperson that does not take the care to ensure that their appearance is in line with the service/product they are selling.

The area of sales we operate in will determine the appropriate apparel we should wear and personal grooming that we should display. The question that the high performer asks is "How will I dress and groom myself so that the customers perceive me to be someone that they want to do business with?"

If you are selling fashion garments, you need to look like someone that they would seek advice from regarding what is fashionable. If you are a real estate agent, you need to look like a professional that they would seek advice from regarding a major investment or who they would trust to handle their most important assets.

'Body art' (tattoos, piercing etc) has become fashionable. Before you indulge your whim of getting a visible piece of body art, ask yourself, "Is this going to be a disadvantage to my appearance as a salesperson?" If the answer is no, or indeed, it assists you dealing with customers who are similarly adorned, then go right ahead. Having said that, remember that many such body art items are permanent. If the fashions change and body art is no longer acceptable in your line of business, you may be at a disadvantage.

If you are in doubt about how you should appear, seek the advice of a professional advisor. If nothing else, look at the professionals in your line of business who are highly successful and work to appear as they do in a similar, unique to you, manner.

NOTES:

---

4. I know there is no straight line to success

Sales is the highest paid hard work and the lowest paid easy work there is. If success was straight forward it would not attract the high level of earnings that are available for the successful salespeople.

History is rich with examples of people in all walks of life that have become highly successful, but only after many attempts. These people have endured significant hardship and continually worked to overcome seemingly impossible barriers to them being successful. Read the stories of Thomas Edison, Mahatma Ghandi, Abraham Lincoln and so many others that ultimately were successful but only after many attempts and apparent failures. These people had no 'straight line' to success. Their paths were a frustrating 'roller coaster' that at times appeared to be taking them away from their goal rather than progressing them toward it. Becoming a successful salesperson is no different.

Many successful salespeople begin their careers being a technical/subject matter expert in a particular discipline. The act of taking a sales role for these people can often mean taking a pay cut to start with in the understanding that once they begin to make sales, they have the potential to earn more based on their commissions and bonuses.

Often the first sales role doesn't work out. It is not uncommon for highly successful salespeople to have seemingly failed in their first sales role then gone on to find the right role where they excel. It is most unusual for someone to take on a sales role and then proceed in a 'straight line' manner to being a sales superstar. Even when it seems that you have 'made it', there are ups and downs from time to time often due to changing market conditions, economic downturns or other circumstances that are not directly under the control of the salesperson.

The salesperson that will succeed is the one that understands that the road to success has many twists and turns, then applies themselves with determination, energy and skill to endure and win.

NOTES:

5. It is my duty to help my customers to address their needs with my offering

One of the greatest inhibitors to success in sales is self-doubt. There are 'little voices' we all carry with us that provide 'self-speak'. Things like: "What if no one wants to buy what I have to offer?" "No one will pay that much for my offering!" "If I try to sell this to them, they will just tell me to go away." No doubt you can add many more to these examples but you get the idea.

You took this current sales role because you could see the value in the offering, right? (If the answer to that question is "I am just doing this to get by" then perhaps you need to reconsider and go sell something that you believe in or reconsider whether sales is right for you).

Your offering has real benefits that address the appropriate customers' wants and satisfy their needs. Without you selling to them, how are they going to gain access to having their wants satisfied and their needs met?

It is your duty to seek out the appropriate customers, make contact with them and introduce your offering. You owe it to them. They may be new customers, or existing customers that you can introduce to an exciting new offering that will address their needs or wants. It is your duty as a professional to work with them to identify their underlying motivations that will range from 'must haves' through to 'fulfilling dreams' and help them to address these with your offering.

In a recent Australian bush fire, the insurance council indicated that 10% of the people that had their houses totally destroyed had no insurance at all. A further 40% were underinsured. There were over 70 houses destroyed. How would you feel if you had approached these people and failed to convince them that they needed appropriate insurance? In an interview, one lady who appeared to be close to retirement stated "We worked our whole lives to achieve this life style and we are now back to the very start again". This is tragic. At her age, she does not have the time to rebuild the wealth that has now been destroyed. A professional salesperson could have consulted with this lady, determined her needs and saved her from this disastrous situation by assisting her to be adequately covered.

What are you waiting for, contact your prospects that need your advice NOW and tell them I recommended that you call!

NOTES:

---

6. My reputation is my greatest asset

No doubt you have heard the old joke about salespeople:

Q: "How do you know when a salesperson is lying?"

A: "Their lips are moving"

The problem is that a minority of members of the sales profession have brought this derogatory perspective upon the entire profession by seeking to increase their commission payments through selling by any means possible rather than holding ethical behaviour as paramount.

The good news is that you can use this negative attitude toward salespeople to your advantage by building a strong reputation as a professional that adds significant value with ethics that are beyond reproach.

In making any approach or decision regarding sales, the first question must be "How will my behaviour strengthen my reputation whilst providing my customer with a valuable solution to their needs?"

If an action will strengthen your reputation as being highly ethical, you should put all of your energy into it. If the action risks damaging your reputation, you should walk away.

The poor reputation that the sales profession has gained, to a large extent, stems from the 'push' approach to selling. Much of the negative perception toward sales relates to the old truism of "He/she can sell ice to Eskimos" where it is believed that to sell something it is necessary to talk hard and fast then trick the unsuspecting person into buying the offering, even if they don't need or want it - or worse, they cannot afford it.

There is another truism that is highly accurate: "Nothing happens until someone sells something". The reality is that people very often rely on professional salespeople to assist them to acquire the goods and services that they need. The difficulty the buying public has is identifying the salespeople that they can trust. To identify these ethical salespeople, buyers rely on referrals from their personal network, including social media, where recommending a salesperson relies on them having an excellent reputation.

The ethical salesperson sells to people based on their needs/wants and, as far as they can ascertain it, the customers' capacity for them to be able to afford to purchase.

Ensuring that you have an excellent reputation, with customers that provide great referrals, is imperative for you to be a high achieving salesperson with a bright future – and to being able to sleep soundly at night.

NOTES:

---

7. Making Target is to be celebrated; having a full pipeline is true happiness

Whatever your target isand over what period, achieving the target is worthy of celebration. Celebration allows us to revitalise ourselves in the knowledge that we can do what we set out to do as well as releasing pent up energy that comes with striving for a tough goal.

Achieving your personal goals or reaching your targets that are set for you as part of your employment should form the basis of celebration and reflection on what it was that underpinned the success. The pressure of selling is relentless and all too often there does not seem to be enough time to pause, celebrate and reflect. It is essential to do so.

Celebrating rejuvenates the soul. If you are not doing this to be happy, then why are you in sales? Without becoming self-indulgent, taking time to enjoy 'the moment' is essential. It is even more meaningful when this celebration includes others that contributed to your success, especially your significant other and loved ones.

Reflecting provides time to analyse events and identify what is working, what could have been improved and what should be avoided. We are conditioned to analyse what went wrong, then try to fix it. To accelerate success in sales, it is essential to identify what works and what went right so that we can then go about doing more such actions.

Whilst we celebrate and reflect, it is important to note that achieving the target and our personal goal is only a milestone along the ongoing road to success. We have to be wary of the trap of working hard toward a target, achieving it and then celebrating it only to find that we have exhausted all of our opportunities and are now 'back at square one'.

Ongoing happiness in sales comes from continually working toward your targets and achieving them in the knowledge that you have ample opportunities in your pipeline that will cover your targets at any given time.

To achieve this, the 'high achievers' are constantly prospecting, developing, closing and reengaging to make sure that they not only make their next target but know well in advance how they are going to make future targets.

A healthy pipeline makes for a happy sales life!
NOTES:

8. I love being in sales because I address people's needs

Selling is one of the professions where you get to address people's true needs. Even where your offering is seemingly a 'nice to have', you are assisting the customer with needs that may be deep seated. For example, if you sell fancy clothes, these may assist your customers with their self-esteem which they can then build upon to achieve their own success/happiness.

The fact that your customers will make a decision to purchase something demonstrates that they have a want that is founded in a perceived personal need, even if it is simply to own or deploy your product or service. The exception to this is where your offering is clearly detrimental to their wellbeing. You need to determine if you can justify selling people your offering if you know it may be detrimental to them and make the appropriate adjustment to your career if your involvement is at odds with your personal ethics.

You may be selling a complicated piece of machinery to a production manager. He doesn't personally need the machine but on a personal basis, he needs the machine to address a commercial problem so that his position is secure or perhaps by solving the problem at hand, his career is enhanced.

The professional salesperson spends the necessary time to uncover the true need of the prospective customer. You may be selling cosmetics in a shop. In your questioning of the customer, you identify that they have a cupboard full of other cosmetics at home. In your continued qualification, you identify that they need this particular cosmetic because they don't have anything with its unique qualities and that they need it to prepare for a very important job interview. By properly investigating the customers' needs, you move from being a cosmetic salesperson to a trusted service provider that is assisting this person with their career.

High achieving salespeople work relentlessly to identify the needs of their customers and love being in sales because they know that by assisting their prospective clients to match their offering to the clients' needs, they are providing a valuable service.

NOTES:

9. I look in the mirror to find out who is responsible

Things go wrong in selling. Things go wrong a lot and all too often.

Orders are delivered incorrectly. Customers change their minds for no apparent reason. Our presentation materials are not accurate. Our pricing is not what the customer wants. We have to spend too much time on reporting and not enough on selling, our key contact at the customer company resigns and we have to re-establish our relationship with a new person....and on it goes.

Average salespeople look for others to blame when things go wrong. The "It's not my fault!" syndrome translates to "Who can I blame?"

The high performing sales professional analyses every adverse situation and ask themselves "What could I have done to avoid that?" and closely follow that up with "How will I make sure that doesn't happen again?" or "I see the situation, how do I turn this to my advantage?" They look in the mirror to see the person responsible for the situation, whether they were at the root cause of the problem or whether they are responsible for devising a method to address it.

Customers are well aware that things go wrong. I once had a very senior customer in a major bank tell me that he has the highest respect not for his suppliers that provide working solutions, but for those that effectively address major issues when they go wrong. We had supplied a solution that was at the core of their online banking. It did not work properly and we were looking 'down the barrel' of a disaster. By marshalling the team, which included the customer, we were able to turn the system around and build a system for the customer that was the best available in their market.

To achieve this excellent result, rather than going on a 'witch hunt' for who made the errors, under the leadership of the professional services manager and the account executive fully supported by their most senior management, every member of the team took responsibility to identify the root cause of the problem, resolve the issues and then to work tirelessly to deliver the best solution.

When it is appropriate, without being vain, it is also important to look in the mirror and recognise the person that made things go right so that you can work out how you apply what you did to create more successes.

NOTES:

10. I mentor others toward achieving their full potential

Being a mentor is a high value activity no matter what stage you are at in your development or career. Even as a 'rookie' salesperson, there may be others in your organisation that you can mentor based on your experience. This may be in areas that are outside of the work environment.

It is not exactly clear how mentoring others provides monetary value to the mentor, but for some strange reason it does. Perhaps it is the fact that the mentor has to think about things at a deeper level and at times do further research to provide mentorship. This in turn provides them with a more structured view on the particular topics that arise and their research is a means of self-education that can be leveraged 'on the job'.

It may be that providing mentorship increases self-esteem and confidence which is then reflected in a greater willingness to strive for greater goals.

Whether the returns to the mentor are monetary or altruistic, they will benefit both the person being mentored and the mentor.

Mentorship may take several forms. For example, it may be a casual arrangement where you talk with another person who values your input on a specific topic such as sales technique or presentation skills. Such relationships may not be seen as formal mentoring but more of a friendly working relationship.

It may be a friendship that develops outside the workplace where broader topics are discussed such as personal issues or financial matters along with work related topics.

Formal mentoring may be entered into where the mentor is paid for their service with set times allocated on a regular basis. The topics will be formally agreed and discussed. Tasks may be set where the person being mentored does research and discusses how the information discovered can be applied to their situation.

A great source of mentoring is referring others to your catalogue of reading/listening/watching biographies and literature written about or by leaders in their field. By referring others to your sources of knowledge/inspiration, you are giving them access to model themselves, for example, on a great leader or successful business person will add significantly to their success.

NOTES:

11. Peers see me as a leader in sales excellence

Having strong self-confidence and achieving sales targets are key attributes of the sales professional. The salesperson that wants to continue to be at their best strives to adopt new ways. They use innovative method and are always ready to try something 'a little different' with a pioneering spirit.

These highly successful salespeople are quick to share their innovation experiences whether the outcomes are either good or if they did not meet expectations.

In their pioneering they discover new methods that work well, often with spectacular results. These spectacular results fast track them toward and beyond their targets. They are quick to share these new methods with their fellow team mates to assist them with their success. Similarly, when they attempt at a new method that does not work well, they are quick to cease using those methods, discover why they didn't work and to share the experiences so that the others save time and energy by not pursuing the failed methods.

By being innovative and sharing their experiences, they are viewed by their peers as a leader, always working toward excellence in sales. They gain the benefit of great results and the rest of the team gain from adopting and melding them to their situation.

The sales professional makes the time available to share their methods that are successful with the rest of their team. This may be formal presentations at a sales meeting or less formal discussion whether that is within or outside of business hours. Discussing the opportunities that others are working on and providing input on how successful methods that the sales professional has used can be applied to those opportunities is an excellent way to demonstrate sales leadership.

At one stage in my sales career, one of the professional salespeople wrote an excellent tender response with innovate presentation and content. By sharing it, the team were able to leverage the winning document for their respective tender responses, each innovating then sharing their documents. This resulted in a massive increase in sales for the each of the team and for the company. The sales professional that wrote the initial document demonstrated true leadership that was gratefully recognised by the team.

NOTES:

12. I read, listen and watch every day to improve myself and my sales capability

The high performing salesperson knows that irrespective of how successful anyone is, there is always more to learn.

Every day there is an ever increasing amount of information being generated and delivered in all types of media. The form of this information can be one of, or a combination of, traditional books, newspapers, social media, bulletins, magazines, newsletters, e-mails, audio (CDs, podcasts, radio), video (DVDs, YouTube, television), internet, television, seminars (physical, webinars), trade shows, training courses (physical, virtual) or any other form of delivery.

To stay ahead of the competition, it is essential that the high achieving salesperson dedicate time and effort to continually learning from as many of these sources as possible.

They will not only educate themselves on their particular area of expertise, but will seek to gain knowledge in a wide range of topics so that they are able to engage with their prospects and clients in a more complete manner.

Depending on what you are selling, it is a significant advantage to be knowledgeable about the areas that your customers are involved in. For example, if you are selling to agriculture customers, you will be at a distinct advantage if you are well read in the economic situation that the farmers are facing, how the weather patterns impact their business, any global trends in agriculture, new innovations that are under way in the industry, etc. Customers have strong respect for salespeople that can inform them in related areas that will benefit them with information that they are currently unaware of.

The highest form of selling is that of being a trusted adviser who the client refers to when they have a requirement. The salesperson that is seen as a luminary in their field and knowledgeable on a wide range of subjects beyond their particular product offering will have a significant advantage over their competitors that are merely well versed in their offering.

NOTES:

13. My product knowledge is always beyond what I need to achieve my targets

To sell effectively you must know your product. To over achieve your targets you need to demonstrate a depth of product knowledge that inspires confidence in your customers.

It is not good enough to 'just know the brochures'. Customers need to feel that you have full confidence in your product based on more than simply knowing its features. To achieve the highest level in your sales career, you need to understand a wide range of successful applications and the resultant benefits of your offerings, then clearly articulate how the customer will gain value from them in their unique circumstances.

The high performer devotes time to study their offerings and how they are being used for the customers' advantage.

As an example, in complex product/services sales, high achieving salespeople understand that the sales process continues after the customer has acquired the offering. They stay in touch with their customers to ensure that the products/services they have purchased are satisfying them and understanding the reasons that the customers are happy with their purchase or not.

Where the customer is not happy, they can orchestrate their support teams to resolve any issues. This ongoing engagement with the customer increases their product knowledge based on expanding their understanding of the application of their offering as well as how to address any issues that may arise.

The sales professional gains far greater product knowledge from these post-sales activities that they can then leverage in their ongoing sales efforts. Not only can they demonstrate superior product knowledge based on observing the implementation and ongoing use of their offerings, they are able to add real use examples to their repertoire of case studies about how their offerings have provided substantial value to others of their clientele.

NOTES:

14. I am an excellent time manager

Of all the things to master to become a high earning salesperson, time management is at the top of the list.

It has been said that the only real asset we have is time. Without it, all the riches or personal relationships in the world are irrelevant.

There is one simple rule to effective time management:

Do the most effective thing at any given moment.

There are many texts, courses, systems, tools and other learning opportunities available. It does not matter what system that you choose to use. What does matter is that you adopt methods that provide you with ample time to do what will achieve the required results

Effective time management is holistic. It takes into account all areas of a person's life that makes it satisfying and meaningful. Areas that must be included for effective time management will include maintaining excellent physical health, a harmonious state of mind, personal relationships (partner, family, friends, community), continual learning, spirituality and wealth creation and retention. You may want to add to this list however neglecting any one or more of these areas may be to your detriment.

Highly effective salespeople analyse the past to learn from it and deal with areas that did not go so well; live in the present and ensure that they are doing the most effective thing at any given time and take control of the future by devising and executing well considered plans.

A simple tool to ensure effective time management is a prioritised list with no more than 10 high value things on it that are constantly being worked on. The list must be reviewed and amended, as necessary, every day to ensure that you are on track. Anything that does not fall into the 'highest value' category should be set aside and occasionally reviewed. Interruptions that do not align with the List of 10 should either be spurned, delegated, parked or ignored.

Whilst time is a fixed item, it is possible to create your own time by effectively managing what you choose to do with it. You will notice that the more expert someone is, the more they appear to have ample time to do what they are good at. These experts have achieved their status through focused time management that allows them to be highly prepared in the right place at the right time. The expert salesperson achieves their status the same way.

NOTES:

15. I can manage multiple tasks in parallel and achieve outstanding results

Outstanding results are not achieved by doing one thing and one thing only at any one time. They are achieved by focusing on one outstanding outcome whilst dealing in parallel with the many things that are required to achieve that outcome.

Winning a yacht race is not merely steering the yacht in the right direction to the finish line. It requires continual monitoring and action regarding wind and current direction; setting the sails and rudder appropriately to take advantage of the wind and currents; weight distribution across the hull; deploying tactics to gain advantage over the competitors; ensuring the team is working smoothly (even if it is a team of one) and a host of other actions – all carried out simultaneously.

Effective selling is similar. It is the culmination of many actions that are taken in concert with each other to achieve the appropriate result. As a conductor creates a wonderful symphony by leading an orchestra, so it is with the highly effective salesperson. The successful sales professional knows the various activities that constitute sales success and is able to 'conduct' them simultaneously to achieve outstanding results.

Depending on the type of sales, coordination of many activities will be required. It may be arranging demonstration stock, having technical support people available, introducing reference customers, inspiring presentation of the offering or a visual presentation to the customer and their management. To elegantly close sales it is imperative that the customer experiences a smooth delivery of the sales effort. It is the sales professional's skills at managing the multiple necessary activities that will result in a positive experience for the customer and enable the closing of the sale.

To effectively manage the various activities that are required to sell, a project management approach should be taken. For complex sales, a project plan should be written with the various actions defined and a time line for each defined so that the completion deadline is achieved. For more information on this, read about the Critical Path Method applied to Project Management. There are ample texts on this topic but a good starting point is Wikipedia.

NOTES:

---

16. I offer praise in abundance and criticism sparingly and only in private

Everyone wants recognition for their efforts. The salespeople that get their support team to willingly 'go the extra mile for them' are the ones that offer genuine praise freely and often for good work.

This praise can take the form of direct praise to the individual as well as public praise for the efforts of an individual along with the rest of the team that has been involved in the good work.

Sales support teams may not work at the rapid pace of the sales professional. At times things can go wrong. This will especially be the case when moving Into new territories, working with new solutions, introducing new products or any other of a myriad of sales situations.

When things are going too slow or go wrong, the average salesperson will look to apportion blame and criticise those involved or anyone or thing that may be at fault. In these situations, average salespeople are quick to criticize in front of others and to highlight the issues with their team members' management.

The high achieving sales professional understands that their support team is not purposefully working against them and takes a leadership approach with the team to identify what could be done better and to address the issues.

Where a team member has not performed to the standard required, they privately discuss the matter with them, seeking to identify the real problem. Where there is some adjustment required in the person's behaviour the professional salesperson provides some constructive feedback to the team member well away from the rest of the team, that individual's manager and especially away from the customer.

This allows the team member to retain their dignity and the sales professional the opportunity to better understand how they can assist them to perform better in future. Where necessary, the sales professional can act as a catalyst for the team member to gain education and support from their manager.

The professional salesperson is always ready to accept constructive criticism from their support team so that they can better lead the sales effort in future.

NOTES:

17. I am an excellent presenter and public speaker

It is virtually impossible to be a high achieving salesperson and avoid presenting and speaking to groups of people. In large value transactions, it may be necessary to present to a large number of people, possibly to a group of senior executives or even at Board level.

A clear, well-structured presentation that is articulately delivered may be the deciding factor in winning significant business.

There is a popular misconception that the most effective speakers are 'born' with their talent and that presenting comes easily to them. Whilst there is a very small group of people that are able to present naturally, the vast majority of excellent presenters have developed their capabilities through diligent study, hours of rehearsal and countless presentations to various sized audiences. Many of the great orators had speech difficulties but learned to overcome them and then went on to become icons.

Excellent presentation skills and powerful public speaking capability can be learned and honed using well established methods. There is an ample supply of material available online, in DVDs, in books and by face to face tuition that will provide the fundamentals and finer points of how to be an excellent presenter/public speaker.

Groups such as Toastmasters International provide forums where members practice their speaking skills in a supportive, non-threatening environment. Participating in one of these groups will enhance presenting skills that will contribute to superior sales performance.

There are further benefits to being an excellent presenter. Being a well-trained, experienced, confident presenter and public speaker adds to one's confidence in one-on-one meetings and smaller gatherings. The ability to think clearly and present, both formally and impromptu, is as applicable in person to person business discussion with a client as it is to present to a large group of people.

NOTES:

18. I seek the opportunity to speak in public regularly to improve my profile.

Awareness of your offering is a cornerstone of sales success. There are a range of methods that are used to promote your offering which will range from electronic methods such as direct email, search engine optimisation, on line, electronic media (e.g. TV/Radio/web) through to physical advertising, PR/press etc. With all the methods of promotion being used, it is difficult to 'stand out from the crowd'.

It is here that your personal efforts can make a massive difference to your sales results, both in terms of leads and closed deals. By speaking in public, you are promoting your offering whether you are directly speaking about it or presenting on some other matter that you are passionate about.

Remember, "People buy from People". Ensuring that you are taking a high profile by speaking to people that may be prospective customers or who may refer others that are prospects to you is a very powerful sales development tool. By positioning yourself as a leader, thought leader or subject matter expert in a particular field through 'taking the podium', you are capturing mind-share of your audience who experience you in person which in turn places you as 'front of mind' with your audience, well above your competitors who remain essentially anonymous.

Naturally, you will aim to speak at events that are aimed at your industry's market, but do not stop there. For example, if you are selling home services, be sure to be involved in local interest groups and take a leadership/contributor role of some description where you address the constituents on that matter. The audience will be more aware of you and want to know more about you. Provided that they see you as learned, capable and trustworthy, they will immediately think of you when they require the services you sell.

This is a 'multiple win'. You and the community gain advantage from your input to that local interest group, you make new friends/acquaintances and you raise awareness of your vocation which in turn enhances your likelihood of developing leads/referrals that will convert into ongoing business. Of course, you will need to continually hone your speaking skills, but that in itself is an enjoyable, potential lead developing pursuit.

NOTES:

19. I study the Masters in business and selling

Every now and then some genius comes up with a completely new idea but the reality is that completely new sales thinking is very rare.

Transactions have been happening for thousands of years with some individuals being much more successful and profitable than others. Like all disciplines, there are Masters who have either devised unique methods or perfected proven ways of creating wealth from business and sales.

You can spend a long time and a great deal of effort working to be a major success based on your creative thinking and experimentation alone or you can fast track the process by studying "the Masters".

There is an unlimited supply of information that you can draw upon. People such as J. Douglas Edwards, Zig Ziglar, Tom Hopkins and so many more who have written books and recorded videos on Sales.

Look for works by the 'Masters' and 'new age sales gurus'. Study their works, internalise the key points and adapt their methods until you arrive at your unique style that feels comfortable for you whilst massively improving your performance.

Use all media to its best advantage. Watch YouTube videos, listen to Podcasts, subscribe to blogs, go 'old school' and create your own reference library of the Masters' books to refer to so that you can apply their methods to your situation. Attend seminars to hear and learn first-hand from sales experts.

Especially, take notes. Compile your own 'scrap book' of ideas that you have gleaned from the masters. As you are writing down the key points that you want to refer to, add your own thoughts and experiences to the notes. It is amazing how writing something by hand reinforces the idea in your mind so that you can recall it more readily. Merely listening or watching passively has far less impact than actively taking notes whilst you are involved in reading or watching/hearing a presentation regardless of whether it is virtual or in-person.

NOTES:

20. I have outstanding mentors to assist me in achieving my goals

Wisdom is a salespersons' most effective secret weapon. The ability to unpassionately assess a sales situation and wisely take the appropriate action will differentiate the average salesperson from the high performing professional. The only problem is that it can take many years of success and failure to accumulate a solid foundation of sales wisdom.

You rightly ask "If wisdom takes years to accumulate, how am I going to reach success in the near future?" The answer is to leverage the experience and wisdom of outstanding people by having them as mentors. This does not mean that you only consult with highly successful salespeople, but that you have a range of mentors that assist you with areas such as business, finance, law, marketing, subject matter expertise in the market vertical that you are selling to etc.

For example, if you are selling into the health sector, seek mentorship from a health professional who is highly respected in that sector to assist you with your depth of knowledge which will in turn assist you in your dealings with your health sector customers.

For sales wisdom, seek out people that you respect and who have achieved results that you aspire toward. Get to know them if possible and seek their counsel. They may be more approachable than you first suspect. Provided you do not consume too much of their time, many are often happy, indeed flattered, to talk to you and provide some insights that you can leverage.

You can also have mentors that do not know they are mentoring you. Look to people who are achieving great things today as well as those throughout history that you respect then study them through their books, biographies, articles, videos, films etc. For example, if you want to speak passionately, study Winston Churchill.

Study their thinking; how their actions gained great results; how they overcame difficulties, their philosophy on life and how it was applied to create their achievement. When you are facing a situation that requires "that extra something", reflect on what your chosen mentor(s) would think and how they would act to turn the situation to their advantage.

NOTES:

21. I have a clear, current set of written goals that I review at least weekly.

There is an enormous amount written about goal setting. It is important to study the literature, in whatever form, on the subject.

Goal setting is a somewhat contentious theory with the detractors pointing out that goal setting alone will not necessarily make you successful. I have found that the truism "If you don't know where you are going, how will you know when you arrive?" applies. It can be difficult to devise a very clear set of goals when you first decide to write them down but having no goals at all will ensure that it takes you longer to reach success if you ever get there.

There is evidence to suggest that various people who have achieved greatness did not practice goal setting or have a written set of goals that they regularly reviewed. Closely analysing successful people, in all vocations including sales, demonstrates that these people who "didn't have goals" did not need to have them written down or to review them – they were crystal clear on what they wanted to achieve and lived their lives dedicated to creating the circumstances that lead to their success.

It is very easy to be clear about what you do not want. It is another thing to have a razor-sharp image of what you are going to achieve and a well-defined plan that will get you there.

The successful salesperson has clear goals. They are personal and may be recorded in different ways, but they definitely have them.

The exercise of writing goals and reviewing them means that you have defined your situation and then identified what you want to achieve in the near, medium and long term. Because you can clearly articulate your goals, your mind will work in the background to devise ways to assist you in achieving them. It is not unusual for 'great ideas' or vivid dreams to appear that assist you in achieving your goals.

Of course, nothing is achieved without action. Your clearly written goals allow you to devise plans to achieve those goals and then check your progress as you take decisive, systematic action to execute the plans and succeed.

NOTES:

---

22. I have a balanced life with time allocated for family, friends, achievement, spirituality, learning & health

Unfortunately, life is not a 'dress rehearsal'. <u>We will never get today or this minute back.</u> As the hours pass, they are gone forever. Sure, there is always tomorrow, but miss too many 'today's' and there is a gap that can't be recovered.

Nature relies on balance. For every night there is a day, for every winter, there is a summer, for each low tide, there is a high tide and so it goes. Whilst we are the most intellectually advanced species, we too are a part of nature and therefore we require balance.

Being highly successful in one area can lead to weakness and even failure in another. The highly successful salesperson understands that to maintain their abundant energy in pursuit of their business goals, it is necessary to have a well-developed method of rest, recreation and replenishment, particularly for the heart, soul, mind and body.

Take a look at your diary and see how many entries there are for areas of your being other than work. I strongly recommend inserting appointments in your diary that cover the other areas of your life as well as work.

Be sure to insert times to spend with your significant other (e.g. 'Weekly 'just-us dinner'). If you have kids, make sure that you have time in there to spend with them (e.g. 'Read bed time story' at particular time of the evening or 'Watch sports game' etc.). Schedule time for friends 'catch ups', parties, casual meetings to 'just be together'. Block out some quiet time to reflect and be spiritual, whether that is a formal occasion or just you 'spending quiet time reflecting'. Make an entry to talk with your distant relatives once a week, etc. You get the drift.

The next time you are unfortunate enough to go to a funeral you won't see pockets in the casket. We cannot take our worldly wealth with us so why focus on wealth and ignore the other facets that contribute to a holistic, happy life? Our success in business is up to us and so it is with our success in our life in general.

The only reason that 'we don't have enough time' for non-work-related matters' is because **we fail to make time!**

NOTES:

---

23. I take time out to "Charge my Batteries" on a regular basis

Every athlete knows that if they push their bodies too hard for too long, they will break down and not achieve their full potential.

Sales is no different. Success in Sales requires 'presence' not only in being available for customers when they need your services but more importantly 'in mind' where you are focused and able to contribute. It takes a lot of energy to be 'sharp' and that is what is required to win in the competitive selling environment.

All instruments must be regularly maintained so they will perform at their best. Axes need sharpened, violins need tuned and strings replaced; vehicles need maintenance and tuning; remote controls need new batteries and so on.

The successful salesperson recognises that to be at the peak of their performance they need to continually re-energise themselves by taking time to reflect, relax and rejuvenate.

"Charging your batteries" can take many forms. It is important for you to determine what is the best method for you. A daily, weekly, semi-annual and annual routine is important.

Time out each day to exercise, think and enjoy life is just as important as taking a long break every 6 or 12 months.

The pressures of life will mean that there will be times where 'taking a breather' is not possible but these times should not persist for too long.

Take control. Schedule time into your diary to relax, rest, exercise, laugh, go to the movies, take a holiday, spend time with the family, read a book etc, etc. Whatever it is that you find reinvigorates you, plan it into your schedule as if it is a business appointment.

You can't run a car on an empty tank and you can't be at your best in selling if you are tired, irritable and exhausted. Just as you set goals that will achieve business success, be sure to set goals to balance your life, then take the time to 'relax, re-charge and achieve the life goals'.

NOTES:

24. I focus on doing more of what went well before I reflect on what could have gone better

Most of us have learned from our time at school that when we submit work, we have it "marked". We got our work back with what we did wrong highlighted which in turn made us feel bad and somewhat incompetent. We were then taught to focus on fixing what we did wrong to ensure that we didn't do it again.

The only problem with adopting that approach as the way you operate in sales is that only focusing on what went wrong saps our self-confidence. We end up feeling bad and spending too much time focusing on the negative aspects of your performance. We lose sight of what we have done well and do not spend time reinforcing and learning from the positive things that went well.

Life isn't perfect. No one is perfect. There will always be mistakes and things that could have gone more smoothly. Behind every great achievement, every win of a major tournament and every great individual success there are many, many errors. The people that created these successes took a view that was diametrically opposed to the 'old school' approach of only focusing on fixing the errors. They took a highly confident approach, built upon their strengths, accepting any shortcomings and devised methods of averting errors by 'playing to their strengths'.

Highly successful salespeople go out of their way to reinforce what they do well. They pick up on the things that were successful in their sales encounters and look for opportunities to repeat them. They work out how they can build upon those strengths to put themselves further ahead of their competition.

Where they identify areas that didn't go so well, they prioritise them, fix them if they are really important and work out how to avert them or delegate them if they can. Successful salespeople do not dwell on errors, they work to resolve them, avert doing them again and especially when they do make errors, they 'get over it' quickly' and do not 'beat themselves up' over making mistakes.

Play to your strengths, avoid your weaknesses and delegate to cover them.

NOTES:

25. I can relate current events to my customers' situation

Your customers live in their world, not yours. Many salespeople believe that it is a waste of time reading the news (physical or virtual) or paying attention to current affairs.

The high performer knows differently. They scan the media for information as if they are looking at it through their customers' eyes. They don't just scan the media for information so that they can make inane polite conversation, they look at the impact of what is happening so that they can relate events to the customers' situation.

A car salesperson may be working on a deal with a tradesperson for a utility vehicle. The various trends in fuel price and local availability (e.g. should they buy a diesel vehicle, a hybrid or an electric vehicle, each with their various nuances) will be crucial to the tradesperson depending on where they work.

By understanding the trends and the forecast future of petrol, LPG, diesel, location of re-charging stations and other forms of fuel, the salesperson can enter into a business conversation with the customer to guide them toward the best overall business solution. Better still, if the salesperson is aware of the customers' industry trends they can offer some suggestions as to the body configuration that would best suit the customer to take advantage of the trends.

For example, a carpenter believes that they need a truck that will carry significant amounts of timber. Your research finds that the trend has moved to factory built pre-fabricated units that are delivered to site. You are now able to discuss with them that given this trend, they might consider a vehicle that can be fitted out with easier access to tools and equipment. This lighter vehicle will consume less fuel and have a different body configuration for the specialist equipment/tools required.

The informed sales professional moves the conversation from selling a vehicle to tailoring a vehicle that is a business tool that will lead to greater profitability (and more comfort/prestige – strong emotional selling points), leaving the uninformed competitive salesperson to wonder "Why didn't they buy the truck from me?"

NOTES:

26. True success doesn't demand applause

Many organisations hold sales competitions and heap accolades onto salespeople that achieve their sales targets. These programs are designed to encourage the salespeople to strive to reach and overachieve their targets. The programs provide strong incentives and prizes for reaching certain criteria. They are in the best interests of the salespeople and the company for the team to work toward achieving the rewards and receive the praise that come with them.

The highly effective salesperson understands that to be successful they do not need, nor do they actively seek, external accolades for their performance.

Whilst they actively support the incentive programs, they do not make them the centre of their strategy. They are pleased to accept awards along the way, should they meet the criteria, but they focus on creating new customers, satisfying their existing customers and working to leverage their relationships with them for referrals and repeat business.

The high achiever understands that their consistent achievement of sales targets comes from delighting their potential and future customers.

Winning awards and being hailed as "#1" are worthwhile 'one off' achievements, but every high earning salesperson knows that having a loyal customer base that will provide referrals and repeat business is an enduring asset.

Like the fabled William Tell who knew that to shoot the arrow on his son's head he had to aim above the apple to compensate for the curved trajectory of the arrow from his bow or kill his son, the successful sales professional aims well above their incentive award target. Taking this approach, they achieve their goals, pick up the awards and continue to execute their winning strategies. No applause is required – but it is gratefully appreciated!

NOTES:

27. People seek me for advice and mentorship

It is a truism that we get back more than we give. By being approachable to others who may be less experienced or less knowledgeable in your discipline, you are reinforcing your skills and often 'learning by teaching'.

The successful salesperson sends signals to others that they are more than prepared to share their experience and knowledge. This may be by quietly offering advice on a particular matter or by demonstrating leadership when circumstances arise that may have no direct impact on, or compensation for, them but which is to the benefit of others.

It is necessary to strike a balance of the amount of time and effort that can be allocated to providing support to others. It is essential to ensure that you are not providing advice that you are not qualified to offer, especially when it comes to matters that require a certified professional, however even where such matters arise, simply listening to them then advising the person to seek professional advice can be of great benefit to them.

When others seek to refer to you for advice and you willingly provide mentorship it means that you have inspired them with your actions and enabled them to approach you with your air of being approachable. People will not seek advice or mentorship from anyone they do not trust or that they perceive to be aloof and unapproachable.

To effectively sell, it is necessary that you are able to establish a working relationship with your target customers based on your credibility and their perceived trust in you. A measure of your perceived trust is whether you are actively supporting others being asked for any advice from time to time by lesser experienced team members. If others are not seeking advice from you from time to time, it will pay you strong dividends to work out why not and take the appropriate steps to ensure that you are perceived as 'someone to seek advice from'. Being a person that is perceived as trustworthy and someone to seek advice from will add significantly to your main focus which is to be the most successful salesperson you can be.

NOTES:

28. I have many stories to tell that inspire me, my team and my customers

As humans we don't get very inspired or motivated by facts, figures or details. Even the offer of reward or penalty has a limited ability to inspire or motivate. Everyone has a differing ability to conceptualize details and assemble them into something that is meaningful for them.

The way that successful salespeople and leaders inspire and motivate are by using relevant stories that dramatically illustrate the outcomes that they are working to achieve.

This is not a matter of fiction. It is a matter of having stories that are factual which clearly illustrate the outcome that is either being strived to achieve or to avoid. The more that you have been involved in the story the better as it demonstrates first-hand experience that the customer or team can consider and question. Where you have not been directly involved, the stories can relate to others where there is credible evidence that the story is indeed factual.

Stories from direct experience are highly desirable however having a strong repertoire of stories with real people involved are also very powerful. These stories may relate to other customers or similar teams that faced similar circumstances, then achieved the desired outcomes. In the face of daunting circumstances, providing a real story that demonstrates that a similar situation has been overcome can provide the necessary inspiration to galvanize a team that otherwise would not believe that the desired outcome is possible into action.

Often these stories commence with "You, customer, are facing a similar problem to XYZ whom I assisted to overcome it. The way we addressed it was..." For a team that is involved in a major sales effort the story may start "This sale is very similar to the one our team won for XXX. The strategy we used was..."

Whilst it is not necessary, some humorous anecdotes in the stories help to make them memorable and get the audience involved. The story allows them to form a mental picture of what you are communicating and gives them the opportunity to easily perceive themselves involved in a similar outcome.

NOTES:

29. I don't waste time absorbing things that won't assist me to succeed

Success is all about focus and gaining as much information about how to achieve it as possible. One can never gain too much information that then leads to knowledge that will contribute to the desired success. The greatest issue we face is not the availability of information to contribute to our knowledge but in finding the time to be exposed to it in whatever format it is available.

There are so many distractions available which divert attention from the pursuit of success. It is all too easy to fall into habits of reading entertaining fiction, watching shows that are irreverent, engaging in social media that is trivial etcetera. Of course, there is a need for relaxation however it is possible to combine pleasure pursuits with reading/watching/participating where the pursuit also inspires, educates and assists in the mission to be successful.

Rather than read meaningless fiction, there is an abundance of literature on people that have achieved great things with 'stranger than fiction' stories. Their experiences can be used to reinforce your actions to achieve your desired success. Similarly, with watching television and movies. There is copious content that is highly entertaining whilst offering insights into how you can achieve your goals.

Social media has become both a highly useful medium for staying in touch with people, including customers, work associates, et al whilst on the other hand being a time-consuming distraction that is all too readily available on your portable device. Used effectively, social media is a very powerful sales/education tool. The negative aspect of social media is allowing it to distract you with inane content which consumes valuable time that could be far more effectively spent on more productive pursuits, including but not limited to family, friends, exercise, meditation, education etc.

The key is time management. By all means spend some 'relaxation time' involved in non-work-related media - you deserve the break — however once you have spent the appropriate minimal time, ensure that you are absorbed in material that will assist you to get to your desired success.

NOTES:

30. I study the Great People and learn from their trials, tribulations and success

As we develop through childhood, we have heroes, whether they are fictional characters, celebrities or actual people that we know of either from close contact or afar. Often these heroes are our role models that assist us in forming 'who we are', including our values. Unfortunately, as the reality of adulthood overcomes us, we tend to forget these characters or relegate them to 'they used to be my hero' status.

To gain insight into how to succeed, it is a highly valuable pursuit to revisit the practice of identifying heroes out of the many great people that have overcome adversity and succeeded then studying them in detail.

Many successful people study great people through history and consider them as their mentors even though they have never met them. They often ask themselves "What would my Mentor do in this situation?" or "When my Mentor faced similar circumstances, they did the following..."

There are very strong business leaders, both past and present, who have taken decisive actions to succeed that can be studied and emulated. Often these great people have overcome massive personal issues and used how they overcame them to drive their particular success. Learning about them, how they overcame their difficulties and then applying it in your situation can mean that you gain the advantage of their knowledge without having to endure their difficulty.

Whatever your field of endeavour, there will be great people that have achieved significant success. You may become one of those that others study to assist them, however that could take a lifetime of trial and error. By studying the 'Greats' in your field you are taking advantage of their experience and gaining a 'fast track' to your success by leveraging what you have learned from them.

Casting your study wider than your field will pay dividends provided you can link what you are learning about the 'greats' to what you are doing. Great politicians, military leaders, philosophers, major company founders, religious leaders, community leaders, inventors, et al provide excellent lessons that you can adapt and apply in your quest for success.

NOTES:

31. I am young at heart and strive to be wise

No matter what your line of endeavour, the truism: "The only constant is change" will apply. Your ongoing success will depend on how you adapt and take advantage of inevitable change. How you deal with the constant change will be a function of how adaptable you are, or how 'set in your ways' you have become, coupled with your wisdom that enables you to take a longer-term view.

We are all aware of how children and teenagers have a unique ability to adopt new technologies whilst older folk struggle with them. It is amazing how very young children are able to quickly learn multiple languages whilst as we get older it gets more difficult. The young have a natural inquisitiveness and are willing to explore new ideas, trying out new methods and learning very rapidly. They have no real concept of failure, only that when they can't do something, they have another go until they get it right.

No matter what our age is, we all have the ability to decide to be 'young at heart' by adopting the same inquisitive nature and preparedness to try new things as do children and youths. It is this 'young at heart' attitude that enables successful salespeople to continually adapt to changes in products, markets and the general business environment.

As we also know, the young can easily get into difficulties trying new things because they have not had the time and experience to develop wisdom that will temper their enthusiasm. The successful salesperson continually works to develop wisdom by observing those that demonstrate it and wide reading to learn from those that have wisely guided the course of history.

Success can be enhanced by being young at heart and therefore being prepared to try new ways and venture into unchartered activities whilst applying wisdom that comes from considered ideas and ongoing learning that will assist in identifying dangers that these adventures may hold.

NOTES:

32. I learn from those I consider to be more & less experienced than me

Every encounter with others is a learning opportunity. By asking questions of the people that you meet in the course of business and in social occasions, it is possible to learn a great deal.

There will be those that are more widely experienced than ourselves and those that may only be just setting out in their careers. By understanding them and what they have done or are planning to do, we have a rich opportunity to learn a great deal.

In encounters with widely experienced people, it is important to get a conversation going with them that provides insight into their successes and how they went about achieving it. This is not difficult given that most people are very happy to speak about themselves provided the questioning doesn't get too personal. Even though they may be involved in a completely different vocation to you, there will be aspects of how they achieved their success that you can consider and then work out how you can integrate their approach into your endeavours.

When talking to those who are not experienced and starting out on their quest, there is an opportunity to learn from them based on their strategies to achieve success in their chosen endeavours. They may have access to new technologies or methods that you have not heard of before. They may have a new and innovative approach that you can learn from and consider in how you are approaching your sales efforts.

In the conversation, they may want to gain insight from you and ask many questions. In answering them, you will learn from considering your responses and reflecting on your successes, giving you an opportunity to perhaps reapply methods that you had put aside or to innovate on them to come up with a fresh approach.

To learn from others, it is important to develop an interview approach to talking with others so that rather than engaging in idle banter or talking about yourself, you are able to gain insights into those you converse with. When you get someone talking about themselves, they will consider you to be an expert conversationalist, even though they have done most of the talking.

Being a great listener will make you a great learner and add to your success as a sales professional.

NOTES:

---

33. I admit my errors then work to correct them and why they happened

No one is perfect and it is not a perfect world. We all make mistakes that vary from minor annoyances to major errors that take a great deal of effort to resolve. It has been said that if you are not making mistakes from time to time, you are not trying hard enough because you are always operating within your 'comfort zone'.

Where you have made an error, the first thing to do is to admit it, either to yourself if it does not impact anyone else or to those that the error has impacted. Nothing annoys a customer more than having blame apportioned to them for an error that has been made by a supplier or to have a supplier deny that an error has been made or refuse to take responsibility for it. By recognising the error and admitting that it was you or the company that you represent disarms the other party and enables a conversation about how to resolve the matter.

Great progress has been made with business relationships where immediate admissions of error have been made and collaborative efforts have been taken to resolve the matters.

As a consequence of an error, a joint approach should be taken by the salesperson, their company and the customer to address the issue.

Overcoming a problem with a customer, no matter who caused it, creates a stronger bond with the customer based on the fact that the issue has been properly addressed and that the root cause of the error has been identified and fixed. The customer confidence is not only enhanced because the immediate issue is resolved; their trust that the salesperson and their company can handle matters as they arise in the future is enhanced.

It is not unusual that such collaborative approaches to resolving errors lead to innovations in products and services. Such collaborative innovations further enhance the competitive position of the salesperson and their company against their competitors who do not have the 'track record' or innovative solutions that were jointly developed.

NOTES:

34. I have a verse that gets me through the darkest times

The life of a sales professional is an emotional roller coaster. Even when you are successful, there will be times where "it all seems too hard".

Tight deadlines must be met. The competition is getting more active and your customer has unexpectedly begun to seriously consider their offering. Customers may be demanding more than can be delivered or may be driving to purchase for less than can be accepted to remain profitable. Deliveries may be delayed. The product may have some technical issues following purchase. The services being delivered may not be meeting the customers' expectations... There is a myriad of issues to face as a professional salesperson which all seem to come to mind at 3:00am and you can't get back to sleep for worrying about them.

Dealing with these 'dark hours' is not an easy task. Rationalising may work to some extent but that takes additional brain power which is already being drained by the issue that is front of mind.

Having a verse or two that you can immediately recall will go a long way to putting your mind at ease and allowing you to put things into perspective. Often what seems to be catastrophic at 3:00am is much less critical when you wake up later in the morning.

For those that are religious, there may be a passage from your holy book that puts things into perspective for you. There may be passages from Shakespeare that work for you to get you into a state of mind to address what is causing angst. Great leaders have written many memorable lines that can be used in the darkest hours. There are passages from the philosophers or it may be the verse from a popular song.

A search on the internet will uncover copious amounts of verses or quotes that you can consider. Talk to your peers or mentors to ask what verses they have that inspire them when they face adversity. The important thing is that when you face the 'tough times', you have a range passages at your disposal to lighten your mood and 'put a smile on your face'.

NOTES:

35. I know that I am NOT my title or my job

One of the most difficult questions to answer is "Who are you?" When asked that question most people answer with their name. When asked to expand on their answer, they will very often state their job title and what their job is. Whilst this is appropriate, it is most important to understand that you are so much more than your job title and your job. Certainly, these are important but what would happen if the position that your title indicates is removed or if your job is made redundant? How would you define "you"?

Success requires a high level of self-confidence. Whether you have a particular title or hold a particular job or not, you are still you. In most cases your title and your job are not entirely under your control. They can be taken away from you due to circumstances or decisions by other people. If you begin to believe that you are defined by your title or your job you are jeopardising your self-confidence and may manifest behaviour that others find difficult to accept. You will make decisions and take actions that are designed to retain your title and your job as opposed to doing what is right for your customers, the company, those you hold dear and ultimately yourself.

Being centred and knowing who you are enables you to operate with self-confidence, enhancing your performance without worrying about losing your title or job. You got to where you are because of being you so it is important not to get caught in the trap of defining yourself as your title or your job.

Which would you rather:

"I am the Executive Account Manager in the Sales Department".

OR

"I am an energetic, hard working person who works to support my family and our happy, healthy lifestyle. My values include respect for others, passion for achievement, the highest ethics and 'giving back' to the community. I value my career and work to ensure that I have earned the right to hold the position that I do through my knowledge and excellent results that are due to my customers' high level of satisfaction."

Define who you are, then be proud of your title and your job which you have because you are YOU!

NOTES:

36. I am even-tempered

We all know someone who gets into a fit of rage for seemingly no valid reason. These people are annoyed by the smallest things and let everyone around them know about it through their outbursts of bad temper.

It is very easy to get a reputation for being 'bad tempered'. It is very easy to be bad tempered. Effectively, being bad tempered is simply a matter of failing to control one's emotions. Rather than take the effort to remain calm, the bad-tempered person lets their emotions run unchecked and exhibits negative behaviour.

The problem is that no one wants to be around someone who is bad-tempered, let alone run the risk of being the subject of one of their outbursts. To be successful in sales requires a lot of support, not only from your work associates, but form those that you hold dear and that provide your personal support. Being bad tempered will lead to suboptimal support from others and therefore inhibit your ability to succeed versus the even-tempered person that others are keen to support.

Some people are naturally even tempered whilst others have to work at it. You will know what your natural tendency is. It is important to recognise where you sit on the scale between extremely bad tempered through to totally euphoric all the time. Once you have determined where you are on the scale, agree it with those that know you well. Often their perception is different to your self-assessment.

When you are comfortable that you are clear on your level of temper display, you will be in a position to adjust it to where you know it will assist you and that others will find appropriate. To adjust how you react and work toward being even-tempered, seek out texts or even take some counsel to identify methods that you can use to ensure that you remain relatively calm even through the most annoying times.

NOTES:

37. I have mentors that guide me toward success

Along the way in our careers, there are people that we meet, work with, work for, deal with, whose work we admire from afar or whose teachings we absorb. These people have an influence on us and the way we go about our endeavours yet we seldom take the time to consider these people mentors. Especially, we do not actively seek to adopt them as mentors or request their input as a mentor.

By definition, a mentor is someone that you consider wise and that you trust for counselling or look toward to learn from. Often, they are someone that is influential and more senior who sponsors you and is a strong supporter.

Many of the challenges you face will have been dealt with by others who have devised methods to overcome them. Seeking these people with the aim of having them mentor you so that you can learn from them and then apply those learnings to your endeavours provides you with a significant advantage to achieve the success that you desire.

Mentors offer the advantage of providing you with input based on their knowledge, skills, attitude and the experience that they have developed over the years.

You don't have to know these people personally. There are ample teachings available from great people in many vocations in the various forms of media via which you can experience their direct output or observe their actions.

The key is to consciously seek out your mentors. Determine who the 'greats' are that you want to know more about. Access and consider the information that they have published and that has been written about them so that you can innovate upon it and apply their example and teachings to your situation.

Determine who it is that you have personal access to that you can mutually adopt as a mentor. Provided your approach to them is appropriate and not too time consuming, they will usually be honoured to offer you their counsel and share their experiences. These mentors often become your sponsors and strong supporters. Remember to 'pay it back'. There will be those that you encounter along the way that will value your mentorship from which you will both derive great benefit.

NOTES:

38. I focus on the big things and have a way of dealing with the little things

There are high value activities that will pay handsome rewards ("big things") and then there are the activities that must be addressed ("little things") but which can absorb significant time and effort for little, if any, return.

Clutter is the enemy of success. A key factor in achieving success is being organised to sort through the clutter of activities and determining the Big Things with everything else being the Little Things.

Apply the "80/20" rule to your approach. Determine the 20% of your activities which provide you with 80% of the results you require and focus on them. These are your 'Big Things'. As an example, if you have a territory of customers, you will find that approximately 20% of them or less contribute to at least 80% of your sales target. By focusing your attention on the top 20% you will be able to increase your sales and ensure that they are secured from competitors' approaches. If you get lost in trying to apply the same effort across all of your customers you run the serious risk of losing some of your 'Top 20%'.

Devise a system to address the other 80% of the activities, the 'Little Things', so that they are addressed but do not get in your way. In the example of the customer base, use indirect methods to keep in touch with the 'Other 80%' so that you can ensure they hear from you but in a time effective manner, for you and for them.

Where the little things are administrative, deploy technology to address as much as possible and delegate/outsource any tasks that are not essential for you to personally handle.

Big Things are not exclusively work. Probably the most important Big Things is you, your health and that of your loved ones. Be sure to include these in your agenda of Big Things to take care of them. Remember, if you don't take care of your personal Big Things, everything else is irrelevant. As the saying goes "You can't take it with you!"

NOTES:

39. I truly love my life as a successful salesperson

Successful salespeople spend a great percentage of their waking hours thinking about work. Whether it is how to gain a particular customer, satisfy a requirement they have, gain advantage over a competitor for a particular deal or just musing over what 'making your numbers' will feel like; sales is more than a job – it's a lifestyle.

We only have a set time on the planet that is far too short, no matter how long it may be. There is absolutely no point in spending a great majority of that time in a vocation that you don't enjoy. Best to spend it doing something that you really enjoy or better still have a passion for. It is said that "the day you love your job you have given up work" and so it is with sales.

If you are a 'natural' at selling and you love it, congratulations! Most likely you have glossed over the ideas in this book and mentally ticked them off saying "Sure, that's what I think all the time".

If you are like most people and need to diligently work to be great at sales, YOU HAVE TO MAKE A CHOICE:

Learn to love the lifestyle of being a salesperson

Or

decide on a new career that will bring you satisfaction NOW and into the future, then go about getting into it.

If you choose the first option, congratulations. Now, commit to being the best salesperson you can be and feel great about it.

No business can survive unless sales are made. Everyone that draws payment from a company, whether they are an employee or an owner, can be paid unless customers buy the output of the business. As a salesperson, you are key to providing healthy income and profits for the business that in turn provides so many others with a livelihood.

You have chosen a noble profession that provides employment and income to support everyone in your company. You deserve to love your life as a salesperson and to be proud of your achievements.

NOTES:

Section 2

Technique

40. I have two eyes, two ears and one mouth: I use them in that proportion

The majority of information that we take in is visual. Second to that is the information that we hear and then lastly information that we derive from our other senses of feel, taste and smell that are not particularly relevant here. There is very little, if any, information that we absorb from the sound of our own voices.

So much can be gained by quietly 'observing' the customers' situation. Their body language, attire, the way they decorate their premises, how orderly they keep their surroundings etc. If you are working in retail, you can gain a great insight into your customers by watching how they browse, what is capturing their interest and how they handle the merchandise.

Listening to them provides another wealth of insight into what their motivation to buy might be. The words they use, the tone of their voice, the 'off hand' comments and so many other qualities of their verbal output that indicate how they like to communicate.

Your talking to them should be very well considered, matched to the way that they like to communicate and always seeking insight into how you can assist them to get what they want/need.

Try a mental exercise of working out a relatively easy calculation while you are speaking, then do the same thing while you are watching and listening. You will find that you can think (do the calculation) whilst you observe and listen whereas when you are speaking it is much more difficult. This highlights that you are able to consider your approach to the customer whilst you are observing and listening to the customer.

By only speaking when you have considered your approach, you have gained time to devise innovative solutions to their requirements. Often, the most insightful approach is to ask further questions so that you can arrive rapidly at a solution. This will differentiate you from the salesperson that recites lines or who rushes to fill silences with their own opinions or assumptions.

The high gain in any sales encounter is being able to provide precisely and concisely the right input based on understanding what the customer wants/needs. You can't know what they want if all you do is talk at them!

NOTES:

41. I ask questions, I don't tell

The high achieving sales professional knows that the high value conversations are those where they ask well informed questions, then watch and listen to the prospective customers' response.

There is much written about using 'open questions' and 'closed questions'. There is no right or wrong use of questions, only where they are used.

In general, open questions, where the customer is free to provide unconstrained responses, will provide much more information and enable the customer to speak more freely. Closed questions, where a mono syllable/short sentence answer is predetermined, on the other hand can be very effective in steering the conversation, particularly if you are working with the customer to make a decision.

For example, if you are selling real estate, a valuable open question would be "What is your situation that brings you to be looking for a property?" A not so valuable opening question may be "Are you looking for a 2- or 3-bedroom house?" before you have ascertained why they are looking in the first place. It could be the prospective buyers are looking for an investment property, an apartment or assisting their parents to purchase a retirement property.

In general, it is best to use open questions to gain insight into the prospective customer and their situation and then use closed questions to narrow down the options that best align with the information you have gained from the conversation around the open questions.

Developing your method of insightful questioning takes a lot of thought and practice. Building your expertise in this area is a most pleasurable process based upon the genuinely engaging conversations you will have with your prospective customers. The key to developing skills in this area is strengthening your discipline to stay open minded and not make premature conclusions or assumptions. Especially, it will take focused energy to 'unlearn' prior truisms or prejudices that you may have.

Once you are proficient, you may even get to the stage where you ask questions that result in the buyer telling you they want to transact the business and 'sign up'.

If you want to see a great example of how to use questions, watch a couple of episodes of "Columbo" (Actor Peter Falk), the old detective series and pay close attention to how he uses questioning to solve mysteries.

NOTES:

42. My customers are always happy to offer me referrals

Your best sales pitch is not the one that you give but the one that your delighted clients offer, often to people that you have not yet met, on your behalf.

The key here is to have delighted clients.

We have all been at a social gathering where someone will proudly tell us about their latest acquisition and then go on to tell us that if we are looking for something similar to what they have just purchased that we should go and see their salesperson. By delighting this person, that salesperson has turned their customer into an advocate which will pay dividends to them into the future.

The highly successful salesperson knows that delighting customers with the purchase process is highly valuable. They don't leave it there. Once they know the customer is satisfied, they then stay in touch with their customers so that they will be receptive to providing references for the salesperson in future.

Gaining advocates and customers that will provide references in future is not simply a matter of 'doing your job as a salesperson'. To ensure that a client becomes an advocate and is prepared to provide a referral, you must 'go the extra mile' to ensure that you have exceeded their expectations of value and service.

It is surprising how many clients are happy to provide a referral if they have been delighted with their purchase and *if they are asked.* The high achieving salespeople always ask their customers for a referral or reference after they have successfully delivered the value they committed to provide.

Care is required here. It is essential that you do not take advantage of your customers' good will by asking them too often for references. It is best to build a loyal group of customers that you stay in touch with who will happily provide a reference for you from time to time. The more delighted customers that you have, the less often you will need to bother any of them – but they will be there when you need them.

Deliver great value, delight your clients and make money by asking for referrals, staying in touch with them and asking them to provide references sparingly.

NOTES:

43. I never call on my clients when I know it will annoy them

Whilst Managing Director of an ICT company, I was at my desk at the end of a very long day. I was quietly working after all of the staff had gone home for the day. I pride myself on an 'open-door management style' so there are interruptions during the day. I was working on a time critical report for HQ in the USA when my desk phone rang. Even back then, it was unusual to receive a call on the desk phone. I did not recognise the number but was compelled to find out who it would be calling me after 7:00pm in the evening.

The phone ringing had already shattered my train of thought that related to reporting the quarter's results. Getting this report wrong had the potential to jeopardize the livelihood of not only me but many of my team in the country.

The call was from a salesperson whose opening remark was "I knew I would find you there at this time..." The call was from someone I had casually met and given my business card which had my direct number on it. I am happy to provide my number provided people respect its use. The call did not relate to any important transaction that we were engaged in and was effectively a prospecting call.

I was not happy to get that call in my 'personal time'. I was even less happy that the salesperson took advantage of me sharing my direct number and calling me at a time that I would not be at my desk waiting for a 'cold call'.

There are times when clients need their space. By all means use forethought to work out an effective time to get in touch with them but make sure that you identify with them the times that they hate to be bothered.

With all the media available today, it is even more important to identify when/how it will be appropriate to approach your customers and prospects. Social media is not a vehicle to 'cold call' people. Mobile phones must be treated as available during business hours or for use for highly necessary calls out of hours.

We are all annoyed when we get interrupted by a door to door salesperson or tele-salesperson in the middle of our dinner because 'they know we will be there'. Calling on people when it will annoy them means that you will not make a sale on that call. Worse, it means that you will most likely not be dealing with them in future - which is what happened to my annoying caller.

NOTES:

44. I only sell what I am passionate about

We have all heard of the legendary salesperson that can 'sell ice in a blizzard'. There are people out there that can do that. If you find one, you will most likely find that they are passionate about ice.

It is possible to sell products and services that you are not passionate about but why spend your life representing something that does not make you feel fulfilled?

Having spent many years selling information and communications technology (ICT) and services, I understand that the products are basically boring if all you see is hardware, software and the services that are necessary to make them work. What I find exciting about technology in general is what it enables people to do. Imagine a robot doing a remote eye operation under the skilful hand of a surgeon in another country? That is inspiring and worth being passionate about.

I also spent a couple of years as a highly successful real estate salesperson. At the time I didn't like it because I found introducing people to property and doing the paperwork boring. It was only after I left real estate that I realized that I was successful because I was assisting my customers with a whole new lifestyle. In retrospect, it was that aspect that I found exciting which lead to my success.

In assessing what you are passionate about selling, look beyond the product/service and understand if you are passionate about the benefit it provides for your customers.

People buy based on their emotions and then use logic to justify their decision. Dealing with a salesperson that is passionate about their offering gives the client the opportunity to get involved in the offering with a person that has their emotions in tune with the offering. That is very powerful for both parties.

Highly successful salespeople have a passion for their overall offerings, especially the value that they bring to the customer. Because of their passion for their offering, they are more knowledgeable on their offering than the less involved salespeople don't. They talk to their prospects on a different level. They go home feeling refreshed after a day's work, not exhausted, because they have been involved in something that they are passionate about, knowing that they have helped someone else gain real value from what they bought.

NOTES:

45. I know the trick is that there is no trick in selling

No doubt when you picked up this book, you thought "I wonder what new trick this book might offer?" If you gain nothing else from this book, you will save a lot of time and effort by understanding that there is no "trick" to selling!

Being successful in sales requires hard work to understand your offering, know what its value is to the appropriate market and then going about getting customers to adopt the offering and benefit from the value it provides. This can be summed up by saying that, if there is a "trick" it is ***"The harder I work and think, the luckier I get"***.

Due to the unscrupulous practices of too many salespeople, the buying public has become wary of salespeople because they don't want to be 'tricked into buying'. People buy for their reasons, not those of the salesperson.

There are prospective customers that will succumb to a slick sales pitch and walk away having purchased something that they never intended or could realistically afford to buy. Rarely does such a sale reflect well on the salesperson, their company or their product. After the event, the customer feels 'duped'. 'Buyer's remorse' is a very real factor that all salespeople have to manage, even if the transaction makes perfect sense for the customer. If the purchaser has been 'tricked' into, or succumbed to 'the hard sell' for a transaction that made no sense for them, the ramifications could be severe due to derogatory 'word of mouth' by the customer in the market or even action via a Consumer Protection Government authority.

The old maxim of "close early, close often and close hard" has caused sales to gain a bad reputation. Asking prospective customers to purchase or forcefully assuming that they will buy (the "Assumptive Close") before they properly understand how the offering will benefit them is a fast way to cut a sales career short.

The high earning sales professionals know that selling is based on identifying the customers' wants, their underlying needs and then providing solutions that delight them both at the time of purchase and on into the future. Their 'trick' to making huge sales is to ensure that their clients never feel there was any 'trick' in getting them involved in the purchase, rather, that they get honest, outstanding value every time they deal with that salesperson.

NOTES:

46. Customers buy for their reasons, not mine

No matter what service or product you are selling, the person that is the ultimate purchase decision maker has their own personal reasons to make the purchase. Their reasons to buy are not necessarily the reasons that you present.

Irrespective of whether this is an 'off the shelf' $1 retail transaction or a $1bn infrastructure contract, underpinning each purchase you will find people basing their decision to buy on at least one of their perceived needs that range from 'basics' such as survival through to fulfilling their dreams. For a deeper understanding of what motivates people, read about Maslow's Hierarchy of Needs in any good Marketing text (1) or on Wikipedia (2).

Making uninformed assumptions about the reasons why a customer will purchase is a quick way to lose a sale, no matter how big that transaction is. Presenting your assumed 'reasons' can be counterproductive and drive them away. A sales professional does not make any assumptions and takes the time to identify the customers' reasons to make a purchase before they even present the solutions' features, functions and benefits. They know that they must frame these from the purchasers' point of view, not theirs.

Imagine a salesperson highlighting why you should buy a piece of clothing because of its wonderful hue of red when in fact you hate red and don't believe it is appropriate to wear to the funeral you must attend?

You may be a senior executive charged with leading the project to identify a solution for a highly sensitive, billion-dollar infrastructure build. You are compelled to sit through interminable presentations on technical specifications as to how proposed solutions will address the project specification. In reality, you are anxious that recommending a solution that fails will result in your career being terminated. Alternatively, the success of the project will mean that you are on the way to realising your desire to be CEO of the company. Any vendor that identifies your personal needs and addresses them as well as the technical requirements has a stronger likelihood of being awarded the business.

Identifying the customers' reasons to buy first, then tailoring every communication toward addressing those reasons will pay huge dividends.

NOTES:

47. I continually ask questions until I identify the customers' true needs

As the saying goes "everything is not always as it seems".

Potential clients may want a particular item. Even they may not know what their true <u>need</u> is. The sales professional understands that the best sale is one where not only does the purchase address the customers' wants, it also addresses their needs. The client will be happy with the purchase and continue to be happy after the 'euphoria' of the purchase wears off. This leads to referrals and repeat sales which is where the high profit sales are.

A well-planned line of questioning to identify the needs of customers is highly valuable. This moves the salesperson into the position of being a consultant who is assisting their clients with a true solution. It is also an opportunity to increase the value of the transaction by providing the customer with a better-quality item and to you by selling a higher margin item.

As an example, let's suppose you are selling shoes. A lady asks to try on a particular pair. Whilst you are getting the shoes she requests, you ask "What will you be doing whilst wearing the shoes?" She lets you know that she is a sales executive and the shoes are for work purposes. You realize that these shoes are stylish but will become uncomfortable if worn all day. You then recommend that she try on another pair of shoes that are well cushioned, very stylish and of high quality. You inform her that whilst these are more expensive, they will last twice as long as the ones she has asked for whilst retaining their new look. You let her know that given the cushioning and quality, you have had other customers tell you that when they wear these shoes, their feet and legs are far less tired at the end of the day. Your close is "These are a sounder investment provided you like the style". If she buys them, you have done her a service. If she goes with the cheaper shoes and they don't suit her, she knows that you advised her against those shoes. Either way, she is likely to be a return customer.

The practice of asking meaningful questions to identify the client's true need, then offering a well-rounded solution, increases customer satisfaction, delivers repeat business and makes it much harder for a competitor who just 'sells' based on apparent needs.

NOTES

48. I don't jump to conclusions about what a customer's true needs are

Appearances can be very deceptive.

A man dressed in attire that made him appear to be a tradesperson walked into an irrigation system supplier and asked the attendant to direct him to the area where the fittings were for garden watering equipment. The attendant pointed him in the direction of the equipment assuming the man, being a tradesman, knew what he needed. The attendant then turned to another person who was not dressed as a tradesperson and began serving them. They required a lot of assistance which meant the attendant was busy for an extended time. All the other attendants were likewise engaged with customers.

After an extended time, the first man approached the attendant, somewhat irate and asked for assistance. As opposed to what the attendant assumed, the man was a factory worker who had no knowledge of pool fittings and needed the assistance of the attendant in the first place. The attendant had made the incorrect assumption that because he was dressed as a tradesperson, he didn't need any assistance. The attendant ran the risk of losing the customer purely because they made an assumption.

Even when customers clearly state what they want, it is worth asking a few questions to see if there is an underlying need that the customer is not aware of. They may have formed their purchasing decision on old information or been incorrectly advised by a friend or less informed salesperson. They may be inquiring about a certain product that does not have the features that they need to fulfil their requirement. There may be accessories that will benefit them but which they are not aware of.

Learning not to make assumptions and practicing the art of uncovering the customers' real needs opens the way for increased sales revenue through providing superior customer service. This will in turn result in greater customer satisfaction that will then lead to return business as well as referrals.

NOTES:

49. I know that customers buy with their emotions first & their logic second

You've done the numbers and presented them perfectly. You have demonstrated that the features of your offering are superior to the competitors' and yet the customer buys the same offering that they usually buy. What happened?

It is highly likely that the customer made an emotional purchase.

There may be any number of emotions that drove their decision. They may have a friendship with the salesperson that they bought from that you have not had the time to develop with them. They may be hesitant because your product is not well known in the market. Perhaps their respected peers use the brand that they purchased and they do not want to be singled out for derision or being embarrassed by their their decision if it is proven to be unwise. They may have had pressure from their superiors to continue with purchasing from the same supplier, like a child being directed by their parents.

Whatever their reasons are, they have highly likely to have bought based on emotions that overrode their logic.

It is important to uncover the emotional aspects of a customer's decision criteria. In qualifying the customer, be sure to talk about feelings, ask questions about what they believe about the product and how they are going to use it.

If a person is buying an item of clothing, no matter how many compliments the salesperson offers, the customer will not purchase the item if it does not make them feel good. Even though the person may love the garment, if they are afraid their friends will make fun of them because it is too far removed from what they normally wear, they will be unlikely to purchase the garment.

Customers will make illogical decisions to purchase because an item because it reminds them of a happier time or perhaps someone they loved. Where the purchase is a major business transaction, the decision maker will decide depending on how they will be perceived for making the purchase. It could be that staying with the same supplier many make them appear to be afraid of implementing change or by engaging with a new supplier that they will be perceived as taking too great a risk.

The astute salesperson engages in conversation to understand the customers' feelings and goes about satisfying them.

NOTES:

---

50. My Sales manager is my best ally at work

The conversations around the drink cooler, the coffee with your fellow salespeople and the discussion with the admin staff are all useful to maintain your support team. However, each of these people have a very limited influence on your wealth.

The one person in the organisation that has a major influence on your wealth is your Sales Manager.

In the majority of instances, your sales manager has wide experience, is authorised to allocate targets, sales territories and ultimately structure the sales team as they see fit to achieve the company's objectives.

Irrespective of how experienced you are, you should treat your sales manager as your mentor. Seek to gain as much learning from them and their experience as you can. Discuss your approach with them. Have them attend prospect and client meetings with you. Seek their input and feedback on how you can improve your performance. You will learn a great deal; they will gain insight into your approach and because of your continued interaction with them, you will spend less time 'reporting to them' and more time strategizing on how to increase you sales with them which in turn will increase your wealth!

A professional salesperson will, from time to time, have new sales managers appointed. Some of these will be highly experienced and some may be relatively new to the position. It may be that the new sales manager is a colleague that has been promoted to the role.

Where the new sales manager is widely experienced, it is a great opportunity to learn new methods from them as well as leverage their experience.

Where the new manager is less experienced or a colleague that has been promoted, it can be more challenging to accept them in the role. The wise salesperson works to ensure that they have a strong working relationship with the new sales manager and supports them as they work their way into the role. The sales manager has been appointed for good reason. By closely working and supporting them, you are able to rapidly achieve a positive working relationship. The purpose of a sales manager is to ensure all of their sales team achieve their targets. Work out with them how they can assist you to achieve your target and then positively engage with them so that you can each achieve your respective goals.

NOTES:

51. I am my toughest sales manager who accepts nothing but the best!

The average salesperson will only do the minimum of what is required to keep their manager off their back and to make sufficient sales to keep them in a job.

The high achieving salesperson sees them self as 'running their own business'. They take full responsibility for their results and do what is required to achieve them within the ethical boundaries set by the organisation they work for.

They know that being a success in sales revolves around setting goals, devising a plan to achieve them, closely managing their time, doing what is required with every minute that they have allocated to the plan and continually checking progress toward completing the milestones that will achieve their goals.

In essence they are their own sales manager. They set high standards, are relentless in working toward maintaining them and are unforgiving when it comes to underperformance.

In being your own sales manager, it is essential to liaise closely with your actual Sales Manager and agree upon the method and metrics that you are working to. Letting them know what you are doing and regularly discussing your progress against your metrics will gain their support. They will be able to make suggestions on how you can adjust your approach to over-achieve your goals.

An excellent approach is to have a written territory strategy aimed at over-achieving your targets and agreeing it with your sales manager. This allows their valuable input into the strategy and their assistance for you to successfully execute it.

By assuming the role of being your own sales manager and sharing your plans with the Sales Manager, you will remove the necessity to have formal meetings regarding your performance which means you will have more time selling. A 'win-win' for you and your Sales Manager.

NOTES:

52. My admin work is always completed on time.

Most salespeople I have worked with are allergic to administration work (which used to be called 'paperwork') and tedious processes. The reality is that an organisation, whether it is a single person operator or a large multi-national company, requires a certain level of administration to ensure that it operates effectively within its governance requirements.

Whilst the real value of the sales professional is in outward bound sales activities, they will fail if they do not pay proper attention to the 'back end' detail.

Dealing with the required physical or electronic 'paperwork' is a matter of time management. Administration activity must be factored into the salesperson's routine.

It must be dealt with the same way as other non-customer specific activities that every salesperson must undertake. These may include personal wellbeing, education, vacations, family/friend time, vehicle repair and a host of other minor but essential activities.

Failure to 'stay on top' of the admin work will damage sales performance. The support team will prefer to work with others who give them the right input in a timely manner meaning that tardy salespeople have to spend more time to get the team to do their work for them leading to less time selling.

Failure to input critical details regarding a sale will result in late delivery of orders to clients and run the risk of incorrect orders. The salesperson will then be further distracted from selling by dealing with the dissatisfied customers. Ultimately, they may even lose that client meaning that they have to replace the revenue they previously gained from those lost customers which will take even more time.

The highly successful salesperson understands that 'admin work' comes with the job and allocates specific time to complete it in their time management system. They know that having an ever-increasing backlog of admin work is non-productive, wasting valuable time and energy to address it when they are finally forced to deal with it. The time that they apportion to promptly 'doing their admin' is outside of the 'golden hours' when customers are receptive to spending time with them or when they are preparing for critical sales activity.

NOTES:

53. I put in the work "up front" on a sales opportunity so that the close is easy

A common sales manager's mistake is thinking that the reason that more sales aren't being made is that the sales team are bad at "closing". In some, this may be true instances, but in the majority of cases of poor sales performance, the root cause is that there is not enough emphasis being put on creating the situation where the 'close' is integrated into the process from the beginning.

Average salespeople "close often, close hard". The high achiever understands that closing starts from "Hello". They work with their customers to create a relationship where the customer gains value from the salesperson and trusts them. They identify their wants, define their underlying needs and then work with the customer to arrive at a solution. It is not unusual in this process for the customer to request the details for ordering and delivery. The salesperson's 'close' is to negotiate the suitable commercial terms.

Suppose you are selling commercial vehicles. A prospect visits your premises and tells you "I am looking for a 3-tonne truck." The average salesperson proceeds to show them what they have on the lot, asking them questions about how much they want to pay, tells the customer the features of the trucks that are in their price bracket, then asks "Do you want to buy one?" to which the customer responds "I'll think about it." then walks out.

The sales professional takes a different approach. They enter into a conversation with the prospect enquiring what their business is, how they will use the truck, if it is replacing a current vehicle, why are they looking for a new one etc. Once the professional has a clear, agreed list of customer requirements they then proceed to advise them on the truck that will best address those needs. It may be that their current truck is unreliable because it is continually overloaded so the professional introduces them to a 5-tonne truck or one with a higher power motor to handle the continual load and better meet their needs.

In this method, the customer engages with the salesperson, realising that they are not merely attempting to 'sell them' what they have on the lot but genuinely working with them to find a solution to their needs. The process of moving to 'close the sale' becomes the formality of 'doing the paperwork'.

NOTES:

54. I know that the best 'close' is the one that is never needed

Much has been written about 'closing'. These are techniques to convince a buyer to complete the purchase. Any good book on selling will include a chapter on 'closing'. Every high performing salesperson will have read several of these books and be able to apply the 'Closes' whenever one is needed.

Whilst professionals know their 'Closes', the high earning salespeople know that the best 'Close' is the one that is never needed.

Customers do not like surprises. Especially, customers do not want to feel pressured into a purchase, particularly for major acquisitions such as real estate or significant business transactions. It is human nature to become defensive when others attempt to either push us into a decision or attempt to make one for us.

The high earning salesperson has established with their customer that they are a person of integrity, knowledgeable regarding the solution that they are offering and that they are working with the customer to satisfy their wants and needs.

In the process of working through the sales process with the customer, it becomes obvious that it is in their best interests to proceed with the acquisition. No 'close' is required. All that is required is to 'tidy up the paperwork' and put the delivery process in train.

Let's consider the example of a highly complex infrastructure project sale. The process to purchase may take several months, if not years. The sales professional will have been continually working with the prospective customer and their organisation to understand the requirements and assisting them to define the solution that they require.

Usually a tender process is enacted where the sales professional will lead a team responding to the customer's requirements that they had already had a part in defining and designing potential solutions. The tender response process will be one of formally proposing the solution that has already been discussed. Provided the sales process has been effective, the 'close' will be formal presentations that make it obvious that the customer should acquire the solution. Following their decision, negotiations on price/legal terms will logically follow and the sale will be 'closed'.

NOTES:

55. I am second to none at closing sales

The act of selling relies on one thing and one thing only: the customer making a decision to buy.

Making the decision to buy anything major does not come easily to the majority of people. Even for less expensive items, many people that are confronted with a choice find it difficult to make a buying decision despite the fact that they require what is being offered.

There are untold reasons why a person has difficulty in making the decision to buy and it is here that the sales professional becomes a trusted advisor to assist them by artfully guiding them and closing the sale.

The high achieving sales professional works with the customer to understand their wants as well as their underlying needs and then guides them through the decision-making process so that they can make the appropriate decision.

The key to effectively guiding the customer toward making a purchase is a well-structured series of questions to uncover their perceived needs that can be addressed by them adopting the offering.

Once the customer has considered the line of questioning, you are in a situation to understand their unique situation. This process of uncovering the reasons that a customer will gain benefit from the solution may be very short for small items or extend to much longer periods for major purchases. Indeed, for major capital acquisitions, the process may be months, if not years.

The sales professional has a well thought out process to guide them toward the appropriate decision. Using this approach, the 'close' to complete the sale becomes a logical question which may be as simple as a statement along the lines of summing up the agreed benefits that the customer has stated and asking them to sign the order or hand over the money. A typical statement would be "Based on your statements, you see that the air-conditioning system will keep your home at the right temperature year-round at an affordable cost with a minimum of maintenance. Please sign here so we can get the team to commence the installation next Wednesday as agreed".

The high achieving salesperson has a 'tried and trusted' method of completing ('closing') the sale, whether they learned it from a mentor or developed it by 'trial and error'.

NOTES:

56. I focus on fulfilling my customers' needs, not making them friends.

The high achieving salesperson understands that prospective customers engage with salespeople in order to address their wants and associated needs, not to become a friend.

The average salesperson will spend considerable time at the beginning of a sales encounter bantering to establish a rapport in the hope that they will be liked by the prospect and therefore gain an advantage. The thought process is "If they like me, they will buy what I have to offer."

Certainly, high achieving salespeople engage in conversation with the customer to establish an amicable business relationship, however they understand that the interaction is at a business level, not personal.

In the vast majority cases customers will purchase the offering that suits their needs from a business-like professional who treats them with due respect in a courteous manner.

Attempting to become too familiar with customers, especially at the start of the sales process, may have a detrimental impact on winning business. Prospective customers usually prefer to remain personally detached from salespeople to ensure that they do not feel personally obligated to enter into a transaction for an offering that does not fully address their requirements.

It is not unusual for sales professionals that engage in long term complex sales processes to make personal friends with their customers based on the mutual respect that is developed founded upon a transaction that provides excellent mutual benefit for each of them. Whilst this may be an eventual outcome, neither the customer or the sales professional will have commenced their interaction "looking for a friend".

NOTES:

57. I never leave home without my business cards

When you take on the role of a salesperson it is important to realise that you are on duty from the time that you leave your home until the time that you walk back in the door, even if you are heading out for a social or family event.

The opportunity to promote your offerings may present itself at the most unexpected times. For example, at social gatherings, conversations with new acquaintances will invariably lead to discussing the line of business that you are each respectively involved in. Often, as you enlighten each other about what you each do, they may have a potential need for your offering or they will identify a referral in their network for your offering.

Whilst the intent of the outing was social, it has become a networking opportunity for both of you to potentially do business together or for each of you to be referred to someone that you could do business with.

Having a business card on hand at such occasions is the mark of a professional. Rather than continuing to discuss business at the social event, the swapping of business cards will facilitate contacting each other to further discuss the matter or for the other person to pass on your card to their contact as a referral.

There are limitless situations where a chance encounter may present you with the opportunity to expand your network or pick up a lead.

No doubt you will have several examples. You may be involved in one of your children's school events or perhaps you are part of a sporting club or a charity organisation. You may be attending one of your partner's functions. You may be going to the hairdresser or simply out shopping.

Where-ever you are that you may interact with other people, there is a likelihood that an opportunity will arise for you to inform others about what you do which will in turn lead to them wanting to 'know more'. Rather than appear 'pushy' by diverting the focus away from the reason you are at the encounter, passing/swapping a business card will facilitate further conversation at a more appropriate time and location.

Make it a rule never to leave home without your business cards.
NOTES:

---

58. I have a 1 minute "Customer Value Pitch" I can deliver at any time

Sales opportunities present themselves at the most unexpected moments. It may a be a chance encounter at a social gathering or bumping into a senior executive from a target account when you are making a call on a completely separate customer.

The high achieving salesperson has a well-rehearsed Customer Value Pitch that they can deliver at any time. The pitch should describe the organisation you represent, why it is unique, how its offerings add significant value to its customers and a 'call to action'. The CVP should only make sense and be true if it applies to your company and its offerings.

For example, let's imagine that you are selling warehouse automation equipment and that you have, by coincidence at a trade show that you are attending as a visitor, been introduced to a senior executive from a large logistics company that you have been targeting. After exchanging pleasantries, you move into your Customer Value Pitch...

"I am so pleased to meet with you. I am with XYZ Automation, the Gold Award winning logistics automation equipment vendor. Our industry leading automation solutions and services are utilised by the majority of the Top 50 logistics companies in the country where they have been proven to reduce their inventory processing costs by at least 20% over that achieved with their previous infrastructure. I am confident that we can provide similar results for your company and would appreciate the opportunity to explore how XYZ can improve your 'bottom line' profitability if you can let me know a suitable time to visit."

The CVP is designed to provoke the prospects interest based on them identifying a potential benefit for them in engaging with you and, as a consequence, for you to gain an appointment with them where you can commence the sales process.

Once you have a well-rehearsed Customer Value Pitch, be sure to regularly review it to ensure that it is current and that it is so unique that it would not make sense or be true if your company's competitors inserted their company's name in the CVP.

NOTES:

59. No matter what my title, I am ALWAYS in Sales!

It seems that no one wants to have the term 'Sales' attached to their title. This is arguably as a result of the poor reputation that salespeople have been allocated based on the unprofessional and unscrupulous actions of various groups over the years who have used any 'trick' at their disposal to 'make a quick buck' then disappear.

The reality is that commerceand hence the general economy, relies on sales. Effective selling is a value-added service that customers require so that they can best fulfil their requirements, especially when they need assistance with the 'finer details' of the offering they are considering. Being a customer oriented, high integrity professional salesperson is something to be proud of. By being such a salesperson, you are providing an essential service to the customers and hence the economy.

There is a wise saying in business: "Nothing happens until someone sells something." Without sales, business can't exist.

The trend to call salespeople anything other than salespeople has seen the emergence of a myriad of titles. Such titles as Business Development Manager, Client Liaison Officer, Account Manager, Senior Account Manager, Customer Executive, Client Director etc, etc. All of the above 'titles' and others that you will encounter are futile attempts to mask the fact that these people are essentially salespeople.

The high achieving sales professional understands that they are in sales and that the title is not important. There may be requirements in organisations to allocate various titles due to the expectations of customers and the representatives who handle their interaction with the company as a supplier however those representatives are in sales.

The high achievers understand that whatever the title is on their card, they are in sales so they continually develop their sales expertise and are proud to be a salesperson.

NOTES:

60. The millionaire next door looks like the rest of the neighbours

There is an accurate truism that 'first impressions count'. The highly effective salesperson applies that to themselves but is very careful about applying it to prospective customers. Not every prospect is what they may first appear to be.

I took a taxi once and got talking to the driver. I commended him on his taxi. It was uncharacteristically clean and in immaculate condition, inside and out. I asked him if it was his taxi. He informed me that it was his and that he owned several others. In fact, it was his personal taxi that he drove to 'keep in touch with the market' and he never allowed any other driver to touch it. Clearly, he was wealthy but loved driving and being in contact with the general public.

We got talking about customer service and the importance of treating people on their merits, not in how they first appeared. He went on to tell me that he once went to 'shop' for a prestigious German vehicle. He was on the way back from washing his cab and was dressed in shorts, a T-shirt and sandals. When he entered the showroom, no-one wanted to talk with him. He felt as if he was not good enough for them and left the showroom.

He decided to widen his thinking and include the very top of the range Japanese brand. Upon entering the showroom, the salesperson could not be more helpful. He went away, considered his options and went ahead and purchased the Japanese luxury vehicle, which was delivered to his home complete with flowers and French Champagne.

He put his shorts, t-shirt and sandals on, got in his new prestige vehicle and drove down to the German luxury vehicle showroom, parking the car in front of the main door. He walked inside and asked for the Sales Manager. The Manager finally came out and asked how he could help. The Taxi Owner said that he couldn't. He said that he was there to help him by showing him the new Japanese prestige vehicle that he had bought because he was treated so badly when he came to 'shop' at the showroom. The Manager was astonished, apologised and wished him well with his new vehicle, offering to provide him personal service if he were to come back.

From the way he told me the story, he won't go back – he loves his Japanese prestige vehicle. He was a 'millionaire next door' and he was treated badly because the salesperson made a wrong assumption without getting the facts.

As sales professionals we must ensure that we properly qualify our prospects. First impressions may be an indicator but the other truism must be observed at all times: "Looks are only skin deep".

NOTES:

61. I know the WIIFM (What's In It For Me) for all of my prospects

Despite how good we think our offering is or how well we are able to present it, we must understand that people buy for their reasons not ours.

Each customer has their own unique motivation that will determine if they will buy or not. There is considerable literature regarding what motivates people that the high achieving salesperson will refer to and which has been referred to else in this book (2). Suffice to say that people's motivation to do something may range from basic physiological requirements, such as hunger, all the way through to doing something "just because they can", like bungy jumping and everything in between.

Success in sales relies on identifying 'what is in it for me' from the customers' position and then basing the sales approach around that.

If a customer wants a red sports car so they can be 'seen in it' and make their friends jealous, they will be far less interested in the technical specifications of the rear axle but more interested in the 'I look fabulous' factor that the car provides. If the customer is a keen racer and plans on using the car to compete in club events, they will be more interested in the technical aspects with the looks being secondary. If the customer is planning on using it as an 'every day driver' but occasionally using it for track days to enjoy its performance, they will be interested in the overall look and capability of the sports car.

The salesperson that sells to the prospect that wants to make their friends jealous based on how many famous people drive the sports cars and how much their friends will think they have become famous will stand a strong chance of making the sale.

They can then change their sales approach for the racing driver to highlight the technical specifications that will ensure that they are ahead of the competition and satisfy the prospects want to be a winner.

It is still the same car, but the 'what's in it for me' is entirely different depending on the buyer.

A 'one size fits all' sales approach is a 'shot gun' approach. Identifying what the customer really wants then selling based on the 'what's in it for me' tailored to the customer is a 'rifle shot' and is most likely to 'hit the bullseye' of making the sale.

NOTES:

62. I understand the customer politics that will impact my sale

In almost every transaction there is underlying 'politics' that will influence the purchase decision. This can range from the family politics that influence a teenager's decision about which clothes to buy all the way through to the country's domestic political situation a government department purchaser has to deal with to make a substantial purchase. We are all well aware of the 'politics' that a spouse/partner has to face in making a purchase that matches their taste but not necessarily that of their partner.

Political influence in a sale can come from seemingly unrelated quarters. For example, a teenager buying a vehicle may appear to be making an independent decision but in reality, they may have borrowed money from a grandparent who will need to be pleased with the purchase even though they do not have a direct input to the decision.

The successful salesperson understands that there may be a political backdrop to a purchase decision and takes care to understand the politics that could impact the sale.

If it is a corporate transaction, they will identify the political context of the purchaser and ensure that they have covered the influencers so that they will approve the purchase. If it is a sale to a couple, the high achiever will be sure to include both parties to ensure that any objections are well addressed.

Even in an 'over the counter' retail transaction, the astute salesperson will enter into a conversation with the customer to identify objections that they may face when they get home from someone that has strong influence so that they can work to avert a return of the item purchased.

Highly successful salespeople understand that once they have identified the politics, they can use them positively to facilitate and even accelerate the sales process.

Ignoring the politics surrounding a sale can result in losing the sale due to seemingly 'out of my control' circumstances. In reality, if the politics had been well addressed, the sale would have been made or time would have been saved by knowing it was not a real opportunity.

NOTES:

63. I have done the work required to make the sale long before making 'the close'

High performing salespeople know that the 'close of a sale' happens long before they are ready to ask the customer to buy.

Traditional thinking is that 'closing' is an act in itself. A common misconception is that all that is needed to be a great salesperson is to "Close early, close often and close hard" to make sales. This mode of thinking insists that salespeople must be well rehearsed at 'closing the sale' so that they have smooth lines to say when it comes time to ask for the business.

Certainly, it is necessary to bring a sales process to a conclusion but the reality is that in the vast majority of sales transactions the 'close of the sale' begins when the customer first becomes aware of the offering and makes contact with the sales medium which for our purposes is the salesperson.

People buy to satisfy their own reasons. The astute salesperson begins every encounter with the clear mission of satisfying the potential customers' wants/needs.

The 'close' of the sale begins with gaining a working rapport at the very first encounter. It is then enhanced by how the salesperson deals with the customer to identify what they are seeking and then actively working with them to provide an outcome that is to the benefit of them and the vendor.

One of the strongest closing techniques is to assist the customer to tailor a solution to their requirement using various components that are uniquely available from the salesperson's organisation. Many salespeople fail to understand that combining the service expertise of their company with the features of their physical offering may be the most significant factor in closing a sale.

Once a positive transaction is agreed by both parties, the 'close' is another logical step in the relationship where the salesperson assists the customer with their decision making, not some dramatic theatrical event.

NOTES:

---

64. I hand write thank you notes to my customers and prospects often

The art of writing is a powerful force. It is said that "the pen is mightier than the sword" and so it is in selling.

In this era of electronic communication, very few, if any, people hand write business letters. It is difficult to remember the last time we received a personally written envelope that was associated with a business transaction.

A very powerful weapon that the successful salesperson uses is hand writing. There is no more powerful use of handwriting than when it is used for a 'Thank you' note.

This may seem like an 'old fashioned' thing to do – and it is. Unfortunately, many courtesies are 'old fashioned' but those that use them stand out from the rest. They also reap the rewards.

If your sales are of small items to new customers all the time then this may not be high on your list of sales tools. But even if you are selling small items, it is amazing how much of your business is from repeat customers. If you want to accelerate your sales, think of ways to personalise a 'thank you' to those people who are your 'regulars'. It may be a 'loyalty card' with your hand written *'Thanks for shopping with us!'* I have noticed that savvy brewsters at café's hand write a 'smiley' face on their loyalty cards with a 'thanks, XYZ' (their first name)'. This provides a personal aspect to buying coffee and entices you back to deal with them, not just to accumulate points toward a free coffee, but to enjoy their bright, personal service.

If you are in business to business sales, a hand written *"Thanks for your time last week, I look forward to providing your ongoing service"* card in a hand addressed and individually stamped envelope mailed to your prospect/customer will set you apart from your competition and ensure that you are well regarded. Corny? Sure, but it sets you apart. What have you got to lose by trying it?

NOTES:

65. I delight my customers

When was the last time you were delighted by someone that sold you something? If you can remember that, what is your inclination to do business with them again or refer someone to them? If you are like the majority of people, when you have been delighted by a salesperson the answer is that you would not think of going anywhere else for that product or service.

There is research that shows that satisfied customers will switch to other providers. Merely being 'satisfied' does not translate into 'loyalty'. There is, however, a direct link between loyalty and being <u>delighted</u>.

Delighting prospects and customers can be achieved by relatively small things. It may be the amount of attention that you provide. Always being ahead of, or on time can be a significant factor in delighting a customer. Fast responses to enquiries, polite manners, hand written 'thank you' notes, additional advice on related matters, personal concern for their well-being and a myriad of other 'special considerations' will delight. The person that remembers your name when you buy your take away coffee is more likely to have you return than the one that treats you as 'next in line'.

I mentioned in an earlier idea that a salesperson that I dealt with did not recognise that the decision maker in the transaction for a vehicle we were buying was in my wife, not me. This salesperson understood that delighting a customer can shift them from being an average to high achieving salesperson.

When we arrived to pick up my wife's new vehicle, it was sitting in the prime position of the show room with a huge pink bow and balloons on it as if it was a huge present. The salesperson arranged for my wife to have photos taken with the car that was dressed up in its huge pink bow and ribbons.

We were delighted. We have referred others to that salesperson and if we were in the market for a car that he sells; we would certainly talk to him first.

How are you going to delight your customers?

NOTES:

66. I am an expert in the eyes of my customers

If being expert at selling is the key to being a highly effective salesperson, the next most important expertise is in the knowledge of your offering and its application.

If you want to stand out from your competition and move to the highest level of success in your field as a salesperson, you need to ensure that in the eyes of your customers, you are an expert that they want to consult with.

Just as we seek the advice of a general practitioner in medicine who then refers us to specialists as required, sales professionals are adept with their offering and its context so they can assist their customers to fulfil their wants and needs.

No customer wants to speak to 'an empty suit'. Product knowledge and expertise in the relevant market will accelerate success in sales.

If the customer has no knowledge of the offering, they will greatly appreciate the assistance of a salesperson that has real insight into the offering, its application and how it compares in the market.

If the customer is knowledgeable, they will appreciate the ability to have a valuable conversation with a salesperson that identifies that they are knowledgeable and who talks with them at their level. Where the salesperson identifies that their customer is a subject matter expert, they can add value by putting them in contact with a specialist or access to further in-depth information.

To differentiate themselves, the sales professional is adept at being able to relate their offering to how their it assists the customer in the current environment with anecdotes and examples of how the offering is assisting other people that the customer is not aware of.

A note of caution. Getting too involved in the intricacies of the offering at the sake of being an expert in how to assist the customer is not recommended. The customer needs to feel that they are dealing with someone that is expert but they will not react well to feeling that they have inferior knowledge or are inadequate. Using expertise carefully and referring to subject matter experts whilst delighting the customer will pay dividends.

NOTES:

67. I can explain how my offering is of financial benefit to my customer

If there is money involved in the transaction for your customer to avail themselves of your product or service, it is your duty to educate your customer on how the product will be of financial benefit to them. This is especially applicable for business to business sales where the product or service you are selling will be used by the end customer as part of their operations to generate return on investment to their business owners.

The financial return to the purchaser on a product or service can relate to various areas. For example, if you are selling infrastructure equipment, the capability of that equipment to handle the load that it is being considered for will result in the customer's ability to increase their throughput and hence derive additional profit due to its purchase.

If it is a maintenance service that is being offered, there will be a transaction and reputational cost to the customer if their production is inhibited due to a lack of the maintenance that you are offering.

Even personal items can have financial benefits to the customer. These benefits may be that the product you are offering is higher quality with a longer life expectancy and hence a lower cost of ownership than a competitive product. If you are selling domestic services there is a financial benefit to the customer through them being able to focus on their vocation which will lead to them earning more.

If you are selling luxury items such as sports cars, holidays or fashion apparel, you can highlight the fact that by your customers taking advantage of your offerings they will be in a better frame of mind which will enable them to be more effective in their chosen vocation and hence earn more. Tangible amounts can be attributed such as "By owning this product, your productivity will improve. Imagine if you could gain a 5% wage increase at work by demonstrating you are more productive based on your better frame of mind" or "Imagine what you could earn if you get a promotion by being well groomed?"

The successful salesperson knows how to articulate realistic financial benefits to the customer based on their offering as they apply to the customers' circumstances.

NOTE:

Section 3

Strategy

68. I am a student of strategy and use it to increase my sales

Continued success in sales is not accidental or merely luck, although behind every major success is at least a 'pinch' of 'luck'. Selling is comparable to chess. Whilst there may initially appear to be only a few moves available, making well executed moves based on a longer-term strategy will increase the likelihood of success, whereas making reactionary moves will most likely result in failure.

The sales professional that understands how to formulate strategies and executes them relentlessly has an almost unassailable advantage over the salesperson that is purely transactional.

There are a great many texts written about strategy. The high achieving salesperson will have read many of them, in particular 'The Art of War' by Sun Tzu (3). Sun Tzu highlights many areas considered imperative for winning strategies including understanding the 'terrain' where you are competing, carefully choosing where to compete and where not to, knowing your 'opponent', gathering intelligence, inspiring your 'troops' (team) etc.

The average salesperson is transactional or reactionary, attempting to sell their offering by doggedly presenting it to everyone.

The strategic salesperson plans their approach, understands the strength of their offering from the customers' point of view, knows the weaknesses of their competitors, identifies the potential customers that will highly value it and then goes about engaging with those customers in a manner that is most appealing to them. By operating in this manner, the competition is often outsold because they are unaware of the strategic sales effort due to their lack of intelligence. They cannot compete because the strategic salesperson has established a 'first mover advantage' by alerting the prospective customer to the shortcomings of the competitive offering.

Highly effective salespeople make it look easy when in fact they have done a great deal of strategic work before they are seen to be engaged with the customer. They do not waste energy or time engaging where they cannot win. As far as possible they create the ideal selling environment with their targeted customers so that the barriers to their competitors are difficult if not insurmountable.

NOTES:

69. My pipeline is the life blood of my income

Congratulations. You have made a sale. Even better, you have achieved your sales target for the week or the quarter. Well done. Now, how are you going to achieve your targets for the next week/quarter and the rest of the year and beyond?

The essence of success in sales is not purely the amount of sales that you make in any one period, but the health of your pipeline of sales opportunities that will enable you to achieve your targets into the future.

If you are selling complex products or solutions, it is imperative that you have a full pipeline of opportunities that you are working on. These opportunities will range from fully evolved and 'ready to close' in the next period down to 'identified' or 'qualified' and require ongoing involvement to bring them to a high likelihood of closing.

Be sure to understand the amount of qualified leads that you need based on your 'close rate'. For instance, it may require 4 times the dollar value of your target in properly qualified leads to achieve your target at the end of the period. Be sure you know your 'close rate' and factor this into what your pipeline must be to achieve your target.

If you are in a role selling less complex offerings or in a retail sales position, you can still have a strong view of your pipeline based on promotions that will be run, re-contacting past clients using your database and other 'lead indicators' such as advertising etc. Your sales may be related to the seasons, holiday periods or some other factor in your market. To increase your 'pipeline' consider making 'special offers' to customers that have purchased from you previously, focusing on particular products/services that are more applicable in that season or to that demographic. Work with your manager and your marketing team to assist them with ideas to help you attract a 'pipeline' of buyers to your products and you.

Do not fall into the trap of being lulled into a false sense of security because you hit your target. Relaxing at the end of a period to bask in the glory of the success you have just had is important but that relaxation must only be for a well-earned celebration, not for any extended time unless it is part of your annual recreation leave. Even then, you need to ensure your pipeline is healthy so you can leverage it when you return refreshed from your holiday.

NOTES:

70. I make my own game and don't compete in someone else's

Remember when you were a kid and you met up with some new kids in your neighbourhood or school yard? They would have games they played and you had to try to understand the game and what the 'rules' were. At times you weren't sure of their rules and often thought they were 'making up the rules' as they went along so that they were certain to win.

Selling is the same. If you are engaging with a customer and introducing them to the value of your offering well before any of your competitors, you have the opportunity to 'create the game and set the rules'. If you arrive on the scene with a potential customer when they are already 'in the game' with your competitor who has set the rules by positioning their offering, you will be like the 'new kid on the block' and spend a lot of effort trying to catch up with your competitor who has already set the rules in favour of their offering.

Work to understand the unique sales proposition (USP) of your offering, then prospect for customers and identify opportunities that closely match your USP so that you can introduce them to your offerings' value for them well ahead of your competition.

You will be able to establish 'the rules of the game' by being early into your target customers and positioning your unique sales proposition well before the competition can present theirs. As a result of you setting the standard, you place your competitors at a distinct disadvantage.

We cannot rely on always having the best 'features, functions and benefits' in the market however, we can differentiate ourselves by establishing contact with our potential customers and gaining their trust for us and our offerings which we have tailored to their specific requirements. This perception of us and our offerings by the customer are the base line of the 'rules' that the competition will have to observe. It may be that we are able to close the business ahead of any competitors knowing there is business on offer.

Even if competition is introduced after we have 'set the scene', we have a distinct advantage to win the business because 'we set the rules'.

NOTES:

71. My existing customers are seven times easier to sell to than my new prospects

It is widely accepted that it is 7 times easier to sell to an existing customer than to develop a new customer. Depending on the line of business it may be 5 times or 10 times easier. Whatever the number, the fact is that existing clients are much easier to sell to than finding new prospects PROVIDED that you and your organisation have demonstrated true value to them in the past.

There is a much lower barrier to engage with them than there is for a new prospect. You have already dealt with the barriers of being unproven, not having a relationship, not having the commercial terms in place to do business etc., etc. The existing customers will have formed some emotional attachment to you and/or your organisation otherwise they would not have done business in the first place.

Existing customers are the most fertile area for prospecting. This is not a matter of continually harassing them to buy but seeking to keep them informed with new developments, special offers and other information that will encourage them to make further enquiry.

For example, the astute real estate salesperson understands that there is regular turn over in ownership of property. Young couples need to expand their premises as their family increases or their careers develop. Investors regularly review their property portfolios. Elderly people move on to more manageable properties etc. Keeping constant contact with customers via simple methods such as birthday cards, season greeting cards, locality updates, etc. will mean that when these people are looking to do something with their property, they will first think of the real estate salesperson that has maintained contact.

It takes time, effort and investment to overcome the barriers and develop the appropriate relationship to make a sale. Highly successful salespeople focus on doing more business with their existing customers by maintaining contact, up-selling, introducing new products/services and looking for other ways of capturing more of their expenditure. Whilst nurturing their existing customers, they continually prospect to bring new customers into their 'account base' to turn them into 'existing customers'.

NOTES:

72. My company makes 80% of its profit from 20% of its products – and I focus on them

Vilfredo Federico Damaso Pareto, born in Paris to Italian parents from Genoa in 1848, devised a principle based on the observation that 80% of the land in Italy was owned by 20% of the population. This was named "The Pareto Principle.

This Principle holds true in most areas where there is a distribution of inputs and outputs and sales is no exception.

No matter what you are selling there will be a set of products, or perhaps a single product line, that provides the majority of the company profits. The successful sales professional quickly identifies the 20% of the products that provide 80% of the profits and then focuses energy into being involved with them and devising ways to sell them.

The profitable products are sometimes not the ones that sell the most. The wise salesperson ensures they are compensated to sell the profitable products, not just the most in total dollar sales.

It is important to have a strategy to apply that will leverage high volume products that have low margins to establish relationships with customers who will purchase the high margin products. If a customer only purchases the low margin products (the 80% of products that contribute 20% of the profit), they are of no real benefit to the company or the salesperson. The salesperson must qualify the customer to ensure that they can leverage sales of the low margin products to open the account for ongoing sales of the high margin products which provide 80% of the profit. If there is no prospect of creating a customer that will purchase the profitable products, it is best to let the competitors deal with these customers so that they experience the losses.

It is difficult to walk away from potential sales however spending time on low profit customers means there is less time available to identify and sell to profitable customers. Applying the 80/20 rule to focus on selling profitable products pays big dividends to the company and the salesperson.

NOTES:

73. 80% of my prospects will contribute 20% of my sales

In a similar manner to the product portfolio, the Pareto principle applies to prospects and the sales they will generate. It is essential to recognise that having a lot of prospects does not necessarily translate into sales and that only a percentage will become sales. Analysis of the sales by customer of any organisation will demonstrate that approximately 20% of the prospects will contribute 80% of the sales.

The high earning salesperson will work at qualifying prospects to rapidly ascertain whether they will translate into opportunities with a future buying requirement that they can address. Where they do not have an immediate or near-term requirement, the prospects can be allocated to the 'keep them informed but don't spend time on them' category. There are also prospects that should simply be 'qualified out' and deleted.

Lead generation is imperative to ensure there is a constant inflow of potential prospects. Depending on the industry and the market, there will be ratios that apply throughout the sales process. In general, it will take 5 leads to generate an opportunity. It will then take 5 low probability opportunities to convert into a medium probability opportunity, 4 medium opportunities to convert to a high probability opportunity and finally 2 or 3 high probability opportunities to become closed sales in any sales period.

The literature is rich with salespeople who made $ millions by 'playing the numbers game' of 80/20. In one instance, a door to door salesperson recognised that if they were to achieve their quota, they would have to increase the number of doors they knocked on. Rather than set themselves a target for end sales, they set themselves a target of the number of doors they had to knock on to achieve their close ratio. Every door they knocked on and got a 'No' response was merely one more that took them closer to achieving their sales target based on the ratios.

20% of a larger number of prospects that converted to sales results in a larger $ value of end sales.

NOTES:

74. 20% of my clients will provide 80% of my sales

Again, the Pareto principle applies to the client base. In most instances, it will be the existing clients that will make up the bulk of sales and it will be only 20% of them that will contribute the bulk of the sales in any given sales period.

Clients have buying cycles and some clients require more of any offering than others.

It may be people that come into the shop to regularly upgrade their mowing equipment (most likely tradespeople), customers that use plumbing services (probably facility managers) or large companies that upgrade their infrastructure.

Whatever the business you are in, a quick scan of your clients over the past 12 months will show that you are making the bulk of all sales from your existing clients (otherwise known as 'repeat business). Of those repeat clients there will be 20% of them that are large consumers of your offerings.

In the example of the facility managers, they will use far more plumbing services than a single property owner. Garden care contractors will purchase considerably more equipment and services from a mower supplies than a single property owner.

This assumes that you do know who your existing clients are, what they usually buy and what their frequency of purchase is, don't you?

It is essential to keep records of your customers using an appropriate Customer Relationship Management system. Provided the system is properly updated and maintained, the data it contains is a rich source of information about the trends in your target market that you can use to tailor your sales approach as well as maintain a deeper relationship with your clients.

Effective capture and use of customer information data is another secret that we won't get into here

NOTES:

...

75. I know Sales success is about focus not being "a mile wide and an inch deep"!

Pour a litre of water on a piece of sheet metal and it will spread over the metal and do it no harm. Take that same litre of water, highly compress it, then focus at a 1 mm^2 point on the metal. The resulting high-pressure jet of the water will create a hole in the sheet.

Success in sales is no different. Following the example above, the 'water' is your sales effort and the 'compression' is your energy. Applying your energy with high intensity to your sales effort that is specifically targeted at a well-defined target has far great likelihood of success than working hard to sell on a wide front.

You may be selling industrial products with a large catalogue of product lines, each with a wide range of individual products that satisfy their own particular applications. To have deep knowledge of all of the product lines, then fully know the 'feature, function, benefit' of each of the individual products is a daunting undertaking. Add to your work load the fact that your territory has manufacturers that make equipment ranging from intricate biomedical equipment through to heavy mining equipment and there is no time to focus.

Rather than attempting to be expert in all of your products and how they apply to manufacturing from biomedical equipment through to heavy mining, it is more effective to spend your effort identifying the product range(s) that you have which offer the greatest competitive advantage in particular customer situations. Once you have identified the specific market segment and their needs that best fit your most competitive products, you are set to then focus your energy prospecting in the narrow market niche you have identified that will be most receptive to your offerings.

By taking this approach, you will have deep expertise in your products and how they add significant value to your target customers. The customers will want to continually engage with you because they recognise that you offer superior service to your competitors based on your understanding of their business and how your products add value to them.

Once you have a strong position in your chosen niche with your specific products, you are then set to expand with more products into either that niche or another chosen target niche.

NOTES:

---

76. The high-value customer relationship begins after the sale is closed

Making a sale is a great achievement, no matter how small or how large. Provided you have satisfied the customers' wants with something that is of real value to them there is a mutually beneficial transaction. They have got what they wanted, it will serve them well and you are adequately compensated for your efforts.

But have you left 'change on the table'?

If that is where the interaction between you and the customer ends, it is merely 'a' transaction. Those that achieve high sales success understand that it is the relationship that is built with the customer after the initial transaction that provides greater value for the customer and themselves.

Every sales transaction is a 'test case' for the customer. Sustainable sales success comes from ensuring that there is ongoing engagement with the customer after a sale is made. It doesn't matter if it is the first transaction or the next in a long history of transactions. Customers only continue to do repeat business if they feel that there is a good reason to do so.

High sales achievers actively seek ongoing engagement with their customers. They look for opportunities to remain connected with the customer by providing information updates, loyalty schemes, special offers, regular follow up calls, invitations to seminars, greeting cards for special occasions etc, etc.

It takes around 5 – 7 times more effort to create a new customer than it does to retain an existing customer. It also takes the customer considerable effort to identify another supplier that will satisfy their wants and/or needs. Changing suppliers can be a difficult task for commercial buyers. Ongoing engagement by the salesperson with the buyer creates a significant barrier to competitors whilst providing value to the customer by eliminating costs to find alternate suppliers that pay them the appropriate ongoing attention.

Developing an ongoing customer relationship and actively maintaining it is high value for you and most importantly for the customer.

NOTES:

77. I spend 50% of my selling time on customers that can buy and the rest finding them

There is only limited time in every day so we have to use it the most effective way possible if we are to be successful at selling.

Whilst it may be entertaining to spend time with prospects that pay undivided attention to the sales pitch and great for the ego to gain compliments from friendly customers it is a complete waste of time if they don't have the ability to buy what you are selling.

Qualifying customers is essential for high performance. The more time that is spent effectively selling to customers that have the capacity to buy, the more likely that you will achieve high sales figures.

Every prospect should be qualified into four distinct categories:

they can buy and will do so very soon;

they can buy but will do so later;

they will be able to buy but not yet and

they are hopeful but will not have the ability to buy in the foreseeable future.

The high achiever separates these people out and spends most time with category 1, touches base with category 2 on a regular basis so that they can be moved to category 1 at the right time, occasionally gets in touch with category 3 whilst sending them information on a regular basis. Category 4 people are kept on the 'contact list' and sent regular updates but no time is spent with them until they move up to category 1 ,2 or 3.

The aim of the successful salesperson is to always be working with 'hot prospects' and maintaining a full pipeline of them at all times.

NOTES:

78. I know who the decision makers are for the sale and have them 'covered'

A lot of time can be lost dealing with customers that appear to be the decision maker when in fact there are more people involved. The successful salesperson never assumes who the decision maker is but takes the time to ascertain all of the decision makers as soon as possible.

This is as applicable in business to consumer sales as it is in business to business sales. My wife and I recently went to purchase a car for her to use. Whilst we would both own it; the car was to be hers and hence the ultimate decision was hers.

We entered the new car show room and the very friendly, knowledgeable salesperson greeted us, showed us around the vehicles, asked all the right questions regarding our needs, what we were looking for, what we were replacing etc, etc. We made it very clear that the car was for my wife and that it was her ultimate decision. The salesperson kept talking to me, seemingly assuming that being the male, it was my ultimate decision. I kept telling him to talk to my wife for the decisions but he kept addressing me. Even when it came to the test drive, he handed me the keys to which I said "My wife will drive the car, if she decides to buy, it will be her decision. He finally got the message but if he had continued to focus on me instead of the decision maker, we would have gone elsewhere to deal with someone that cared about dealing with us rather than annoying us with his assumptions.

The same problems can occur in selling to businesses. If the salesperson does not identify who will ultimately make the decision and how they will make that decision, they stand to be 'out sold'. How to handle 'covering the decision maker' in a corporate sale is an art in its own right and there is not space to cover it here.

Suffice to say that the high performance salesperson identifies the ultimate decision maker(s), how they will make the decision (for example as an approver or as the only decision maker) and then devise methods to ensure that they have done everything possible to cover the decision maker so that they chose their offering whilst aligning the influencers to actively support the decision maker before and after their decision.

NOTES:

79. I know how to use the market conditions to my advantage

There are things that we can control and those that we can't. External market conditions fall into the category of 'things we can't control' as a salesperson.

What we can control as an outstanding salesperson is our attitude toward the market conditions and how we leverage them to our advantage.

Depending on what you are selling, there is likely to be a range of products or services that you have that can be tailored to the market situation that you face.

If the market means that your customers do not have ready cash, look for ways to offer solutions for their needs that will assist them whilst they are able to leverage terms or finance to pay for them. Of course, if the market for your customer that you are addressing is buoyant, use that to highlight to them that by making the purchases now will mean that they are in better shape when their market conditions are tougher.

In presenting your services in a tough market, be sure to break down the investment in your offering to the lowest amount. For example, it is much more palatable to a customer to purchase something that breaks down to a small amount a day/week/month than it is to consider the large single amount to purchase it in one offering.

If you are selling goods or services that are for personal use, be sure to accentuate the personal value to your customers that will assist them to endure the tough market conditions through your product contributing to their sense of being positive and motivated as well as their overall happiness.

A tough market usually means that your customers are finding it difficult. Work out how you and your offering can help them to prevail and succeed in their tough conditions. A buoyant market means that the customers are more inclined to purchase to perpetuate their success or to reward themselves – even if what you are selling is business infrastructure.

Remember the old saying "make hay while the sun shines" and assist your customers to invest wisely while their sun is shining. All markets ebb and flow. The real sales professional positions the purchase of their offerings in the 'good times' to being a wise investment that will fortify the customer in any potential tough times that may lie ahead.

NOTES:

80. My competitors are not aware of my strategies

Selling is one of the most competitive occupations anyone can undertake. The advantage of surprise is significant in any competitive situation. The most decisive competitive advantage is when business is done without a competitor even knowing that there is business to be done.

There are those salespeople that regularly meet with other salespeople in their industries and 'share war stories'. Then there are other sales professionals that chose not to spend time with their competitors so that they can remain a mystery to them and hence ensure that their mode of operation is not clear to the competitors.

It is possible to understand a competitor's strategy by observing the signals they are sending without even seeing them. The astute sales professional watches for signals of strategy that a competitor is sending through such things as the personal contact that the competitor is undertaking with the target customer, the advertising that is being delivered and any other signs of how their sales campaign is being executed. Inversely, the sales professional is careful not to send signals of their strategy and how it is being executed.

Flamboyant entertainment, flashy advertising and similar campaigns send strong signals to the competition and enable them to devise other methods of waging their sales campaign with more intimate contact, tailored offerings and a professional approach that is 'under the radar'.

It is not unusual for sales professionals to be closing business with targeted clients whilst attending major events that are being paid for by their competition.

False signals are a useful tool that can be used to make the competition believe a particular strategy is being deployed to the one that is actually in process. For instance, promotion of a lower end offering in the press may lead a competitor to believe that low end offering is what is being promoted to a particular major customer. The reality is that the campaign is a decoy to cover the fact that it is the high end offering that is being positioned to the major prospect based on its unique features that provide the best value to that target customer.

NOTES:

81. I know who my competitors are and how to compete with them

It is rare indeed to have a potential sale where there is no alternative product or service for the customer to consider.

The successful salesperson makes a full assessment of the options that the customer has to choose from before focusing on how to sell their offering to the customer. A key component of this assessment is identifying the competition and establishing if it is worth competing. If the decision is to engage, it is essential to know the competitions' strengths/weaknesses as they apply to the specific opportunity so that a winning strategy can be executed.

There are many facets to knowing the competition. The average salesperson will focus on the competitors' product/service "feature, function, benefit". The successful salesperson will take a more holistic approach and establish adjacent factors that will influence the customer's decision.

Even in the biggest deals, the truism 'people buy from people' applies. Once the competitors are defined and if possible their potential offering identified, a detailed list should be completed that includes the 'hard' facts regarding product/service feature comparison and the 'soft' aspects.

Soft aspects include a comparison of how the salesperson compares in such areas as the relationship with the customer, previous buying patterns, reputation for quality, success with comparable customers/solutions, reputation for integrity, cultural alignment with the customer etc.

Too many salespeople make assumptions regarding the competition and their standing with the customer. The successful salesperson not only knows the customer's critical technical requirements upon which to compete (or just as importantly not to compete) but puts in the effort to define the important 'soft' aspects then devises a clear strategy to address them to win the business based on a deep factual understanding of the competition from the perspective of the customer.

NOTES:

82. I take advantage of events, no matter how small

Details, details. Successful salespeople pay attention to details and know how to use them to their advantage. Important details include events, both major and minor. Events that can be leveraged are virtually limitless. These can include public events that lead to public holidays, anniversaries such as the founding of the customer's company or of your company, major religious events that relate to your customer or more personal events including their birthday or any other event that they care to share with you.

Personal events matter. A simple call to wish the customer a happy birthday (or congratulations on any other of their important events) shows them that you care more about them than purely taking their money. Similarly, a personal note at their important holiday/religious event demonstrates that they are important to you.

From a promotion/marketing point of view, every event is a chance to offer a promotion whether it be a special price on a product for a limited time leading up to the event or particular advertising that, for example, reinforces your company's credentials based on the anniversary of its establishment.

We are all aware or promotions that are based on the various seasons and have generally become cynical of these. Being creative about using events or establishing events that have meaning to your targeted customers differentiates you from your competition. For example, your competitors will be hard pressed to match a promotion that is based on the establishment of your company. Similarly, they will be hard pressed to match a special offer you make to your customer to commemorate the anniversary of the first transaction that they made with your company.

Look for ways to create special events and methods to use the more traditional events to the advantage of your customer and hence yourself.

NOTES:

83. My network is one of my greatest assets

Sales is all about people. The astute salesperson realises that selling is not only about the direct relationship with their targeted customer(s) but that their ability to sell effectively is greatly improved by having a network of strong relationships.

With the ever-increasing availability of information due to the internet and the burgeoning growth in applications aimed at assisting communication (e.g. social media, web pages, blogs, etc.) having a well-established network is vital for the sales professional.

It takes concerted effort to establish, maintain and grow one's network. The value of a network is only as good as the effort put into ensuring that the people in the network are positively disposed to you and that they are well informed as to what you are doing along with the successes that you are having.

With the expansion of social media, it is relatively simple to have copious names in your 'network'. The important question is "Do I really know these people and are they prepared to offer positive support of me and my offering?"

It is necessary to keep your network informed of what you are doing and the successes you are involved in. It is even more important to provide positive support to those in your network as and when the opportunity arises to do so. As the saying goes, 'If you want to receive, first you have to give'. By providing positive support, the people in your network are inclined to return the compliment.

We have all been offered the opportunity to connect on a social media site with someone we don't know. In some instances, it will make sense to connect because they are genuinely reaching out because of a mutual interest, for example in the same industry or discipline or because they have been referred to you by a trusted associate.

Don't be fooled into believing you have a strong network simply by having a lot of 'names' in your list. Ensure that your network is strong by reviewing it regularly and if necessary, sending a personal note to, or better still, calling those that you have not been in touch with recently.

By having a strong network, you are multiplying your presence in the market and ensuring that you have several people that are willing to actively support you and who know that they can rely on you.

NOTES:

84. I am a student of the economy and how my offering is impacted

The ability to make sales will rely on larger economic circumstances than those that exist in the microcosm of the particular industry that you sell into.

The successful salesperson does not fall into the trap of purely understanding their market and fulfilling the apparent needs of their target customers. Of course, this focus is essential however there is no point attempting to make sales to customers that are being adversely affected by larger economic conditions if you cannot position your offering properly given the greater economic conditions.

You do not need to be an economist however staying abreast of what is happening in the wider economy is essential to assisting your customers to understand why they need your offering in the prevailing economic environment.

Your ability to discuss the current economic situation with the customer and understand their particular concerns, challenges and potential opportunities will set you apart from your competitors who are not paying the same level of attention.

For example, if you are selling equipment to a builder when interest rates are high and new home sales are decreasing, you can position the investment in your equipment to assist them with their productivity and hence reduced costs, thereby facilitating them to be more competitive and win contracts ahead of their less efficient competition.

By staying abreast of the economic environment, you are able to establish how your offering will assist your customer. If your customers are adversely impacted you will be able to identify this in advance and have time to devise a strategy for the sale of your offering either to assist them or perhaps by finding customers that are not impacted by the economic issues.

NOTES:

---

85. I look for advantage out of every adverse situation

Sales is a tough profession. Even when a sale is made, there may be adverse events that mean that the customer is not satisfied or the sale is in jeopardy of being reversed.

Customers make purchases for many reasons with a large factor in their purchase decisions being trust. Where there are adverse situations, the successful salesperson gets involved and works with the customer to understand the impact whilst actively assisting in addressing that situation.

In one major sale I was involved in, the project was severely delayed leading to a significant adverse impact for the customer. The customer stated "It is not that we have had problems that matters, what will count is how your company recovers. If you handle this well, we will be a long-term customer. If not, there will be severe consequences." The project was re-focused and the adverse situation addressed in collaboration with the customer. Indeed, they became a long-term customer. Decisively addressing the issues lead to the opportunity to sell significantly more to the customer on a long-term basis. Had we taken the approach "It's not our fault" or "It's all too hard" we would have suffered not only severe penalties with that customer but reputational damage in that market which the company then went on to dominate.

Although it is difficult when faced with an adverse situation, focusing on how to effectively address it and the advantage that will come from overcoming the situation will pay long term dividends.

Adversity can take many forms. It may be that the offering is defective in which case the resolution may lead to a market leading offering. There may be a personality clash with a decision maker. By resolving this the relationship may become stronger due to a better understanding of each other. The main contact at a customer may leave meaning the sales process has to go back to the beginning. By taking a fresh approach with the new person it may be possible to position other parts of your offering that the last person did not like or properly understand.

By looking for the advantage out of adversity you will be focused 'beyond the current situation' and be able to arrive at a strategy to not only address whatever the current problem is but to arrive at a positive outcome into the future for your customer and therefore you.

NOTES:

Section 4

Execution

86. If it needs done, I do it now!

The Successful Salesperson knows that putting off what <u>needs</u> to be done causes problems down the track.

The trick is to work out what <u>must</u> be done rather than what is urgent. Decisive prioritisation is imperative and to do that, firm goals must be in place.

The test for every action that is presented must be: "How will doing this, or actively NOT doing it, progress me toward achieving the goals that I am committed to?" In order to prioritise your necessary actions, written goals are essential. Having your goals in writing makes them tangible rather than being some vague concept.

An activity list or "To Do" list is a highly effective tool for prioritisation. When a new requirement emerges, it should be added to the list and given a priority. If it is the most important thing toward achieving your goals on the list, it must be done first irrespective of how long other things on the list have been there.

I have found it best to have only three priorities:

'A' for that which will have the highest value if it is done very soon. For example, getting a quote to a customer who will place a purchase order immediately upon receiving the quote

'B' for items that can wait a day or so but which will lead to business provided they are completed soon. This could be getting some information to someone who has made an enquiry, who is well qualified to buy but who is 'shopping around' to get the best deal to buy very soon.

'C' for those matters that must be done at some stage but which have no particular deadline or that won't result in significant business. Administration matters often fall into this category but can become 'A' when, for example, they are required by a certain date/time as part of your conditions of employment.

There will no doubt be multiple 'A' priorities. The way to handle that is to start with the hardest, least palatable thing first, get it done and then deal with everything else which will then be so much easier.

Putting off the 'tough stuff that must be done' depletes energy through having it 'hanging over your head'. Get it done early and it will seem much easier in retrospect.

NOTES:

87. I treat my colleagues and support team as customers

It is a myth to think of the high performing sales professional as a 'lone wolf' or 'one-person army'. The reality is that almost without exception, high performing salespeople are involved in a team approach whether they chose to admit it or not.

If you are selling a product, it takes a significant team to create, manufacture, market and deliver that product. If you are selling a service, as well as the above, it requires others to do the work. Even if you are a 'one-person business', you still need the support of others such as bankers, accountants, your significant other, family, friends and so on.

The professional knows that they must have the support of a willing team. In reality, that team will support you to the extent that they want to. Sure, you can bark orders at them, but if you treat them poorly, they will not 'go the extra mile' and offer greater support to others that treat them with respect and a team approach.

The support team are your customers as much as the people that you are selling to. Treat them as such and they will actively support you and your customers.

Find innovative ways to involve your extended team in your sales efforts at the earliest opportunity.

If you are selling products off the retail floor, talk to others in your organisation and let them know that you are focusing on moving a particular product line. Get information on how to streamline your customers' ability to quickly purchase and take delivery of the product. Make an effort to identify the 'champions' that assist your customers even though they are not in sales, then reward them with a hearty 'thanks' or buy them a coffee or some other small token of your appreciation from time to time.

If you are selling major items/services or solutions, give your team a briefing on what you are proposing and get them to collaborate with you to build the proposal. When the proposal is delivered, let them know and keep them informed of how it is going. When the result is in – win or lose – let them know and celebrate the fact that they all assisted you as a team, or better, that you won!

Your team deserve recognition for their 'behind the scenes' efforts. Convey your honest appreciation and treat them just as well as you treat the end customer. It will pay huge dividends for them, the customer, your company and you.

NOTES:

88. I plan my activities well in advance

Just as an architect sets out clear plans for a building, so the successful salesperson plans their activities. When all is considered, all any of us definitely has is time. How we use it is the key to our success.

Sales figures are outcomes with a large number of variables that will determine them. Many of these variables are out of our control. Just a few examples of these include market conditions, our customers' ability to raise the appropriate funds, predatory activity by our competitors etc. Any of these individually or in any combination may impact our ability to achieve the required results. The one thing that we are in complete control of is our activities that are focused on achieving the required sales results. The plan for our activities will include actions to achieve the results and mitigate the risks of these 'out of our control' factors.

Our sales targets are usually set for the year ahead with subset targets such as quarterly, monthly, weekly and even daily targets. Just as we have sales targets set well in advance, to be a successful salesperson we need to have our activity plans to achieve them written well in advance.

At the end of each day the high achieving salesperson checks their diary for the next day to ensure that they are well prepared. In their diary for the next two weeks or more, they have scheduled appointments, time allocated for prospecting, time blocked out for following up, writing proposals and other high value activities including personal time to keep themselves 'sharp'.

The professionals don't over-commit their time, leaving space for unplanned activity whilst ensuring that they are always doing the most effective thing at any given time.

Having activities planned well in advance means the high achieving salesperson is determining their own success rather than being reactive and hoping that 'things will come their way'.

Sales productivity comes from well-planned sales activity. "Failing to plan is planning to fail"!

Remember the '5 Ps':

Proper Planning Prevents Poor Performance!
NOTES:

89. I prioritise what I will do and do the most valuable things first

The sales professional always has more to do than can be achieved in the time available. They know that a long "To do" list does not translate into sales revenue unless they take control of the list by prioritising the activities and prudently culling it as far as possible.

Every activity must be assessed for the VALUE that it brings with the high value actions at the top of the list. There may be some that you can't see the value in other than "fail to do this and I lose my job" or "I will get a hefty fine". Sure, these aren't making a sale, but they do add value because failing to cover them means you will not be in a position to make any sales or will not be in the right frame of mind to reach your full potential!

Ongoing success is the result of actions that have been taken well in advance. Longer term value adding activity must be prioritised into the day to day activities. Priorities must be set for immediate, near term and longer-term items. For example, studying a business course will not necessarily assist you in achieving your sales target this month or this quarter. The knowledge you will gain from the course will assist you over the longer term and therefore deserves a high priority. On the other hand, attending a targeted seminar may assist you in closing a deal this month or this quarter based on your insight on that topic that you can use to assist the customer to adopt your solution.

Your list of priorities must be set to complement your long-term plan. Ensuring that you are completing the tasks you have prioritises will not only ensure that you meet your immediate goals, but set you up for your medium and long-term goals.

Each evening before you finish work for the day, prioritise your activity list for the next day, ensuring that it has an appropriate spread of immediate, near term and long-term actions. Be realistic about what can be done and ruthless in culling the unnecessary items. Mark

the items that you chose to prioritise with the Value related priority and then **set about doing** them first thing the next day!
NOTES:

---

90. I always arrive with time to spare

You see it everywhere, especially where there are clear cut deadlines like airports and train stations. People running late, red in the face, clearly stressed and rushing to make it on time.

Your customers don't want to deal with you if you look like you have just been through a 100-metre dash. They certainly will not tolerate waiting for you just to provide you with an opportunity to 'sell them something'.

It is not uncommon for senior executives to allocate a specific slot in their calendar for an appointment, then start the clock at the time set for the appointment. If the person that is supposed to be there for the appointment is late, they only give them the balance of the time that remains from the time that they had allocated to the meeting.

Remember:
"Late with an excuse is not the same as being on time!"
and
"You only get one chance to make a good first impression".

Tardiness on the part of a salesperson sends a clear signal to the prospective customer that the organisation or solution that they represent may not be reliable.

Making it a personal habit to be at a destination with plenty of time to spare will put dollars in your pocket as a salesperson. If you politely let the customer know you are there 'fashionably early' you will impress them with your attention to detail and commitment. By being early, you will have time to get your ideas composed, be calm and provide an air of confidence that the 'harried' competitor will not be able to match.

With the productivity tools and connectivity available, any spare time you have prior to the appointment can be used to great advantage for deeper research on the customer organisation, research on competitive offerings that the customer may raise, insight in to current events as they relate to the customer and so much more that can add value to your meeting.

There is another very positive side benefit to always being on time. It is good for your health. By being in control and not stressed by habitually running late, you are keeping your blood pressure down and allowing your mind and body to cope with all the other stresses of day to day life

NOTES:

91. Sales is all about the numbers and I always know mine

The sales professional knows their 'numbers'. These are the indicators of sales success based on activity and the results that are achieved.

Key numbers that every salesperson should know include, but are not limited to:

- Number of calls to identify a lead

- Number of leads to identify an opportunity
- Average number of calls per day required and achieved
- Period to date sales versus budget/target
- Sales by product/service line
- Attach rate of ancillary product/services. e.g. Accessories for vehicles sold
- Number of contacts with ongoing accounts per period (e.g. 1 per month, 1 visit per quarter)
- % pipeline coverage for next period (e.g. High probability coverage = 150%, medium probability = 200%, Low probability = 400%)
- If in retail, Number of customers spoken to per day versus daily sales (close rate)
- Any other numbers that indicate future success

Find out the industry standard numbers for your particular discipline, then compare your performance against them. If at all possible, ascertain the numbers of your key competitors so that you can contrast yours and devise plans to improve your numbers and hence your strategic advantage.

The numbers are important because they enable you to identify areas where you can focus to arrive at new methods to improve your performance. The key is to use the numbers as a basis of innovation, not simply to 'work harder'.

Investigation of your sales statistics can uncover 'low hanging fruit' that you can sell to increase your sales with a minimum of effort/time. For example, if you identify that a particular demographic of customer is dominant in your sales figures, you can work with marketing to devise campaigns and initiatives to further penetrate that demographic. If your sales have a low level of attached services/options, again, you can work with marketing as well as product management or your supplier to devise methods to increase the attach rate.

NOTES:

92. I have a great support team that I constantly reward

You might think that you are on your own, but think again! Even if you live on your own, operate from your home and travel the country in your car calling 'door to door' you still have a support team.

It may be the person that you call to process your orders or the regular hotel operators that you deal with on your travels, but you have a team of people that provide you with the support you require to be an effective salesperson.

If you work for a company, chances are there are a team of people that provide you with administration support, technical assistance and regular product updates.

Know who your support team is. They will exist inside or outside of your company. Be sure to constantly reward them – even if it is as inexpensive as going out of your way to say "Thank You". It is amazing what a small gift or public recognition to them for their efforts will achieve.

One of the great rewards for your support team is being constantly informed of what is happening with you and your customers. Be sure to share your plans with them and to keep them updated, even if that is informally, of how you are progressing.

Remember that their welfare relies on you and the others in the sales team making sufficient sales to keep their jobs secure.

It is surprising how rewarding it is for the people that work for a company to know that their products/services are being used by others in the community. It is common for a production line worker or office worker to proudly tell their family and friends about how the products they manufacture are being used by others. There is a legend of a production line worker at one of Japan's top car manufacturers that adjusts the windscreen wipers on any of their vehicles that he sees in the street if they are not properly set.

It is essential to exercise caution in the information you share to ensure that you are not compromising customer confidentiality. However, keeping the extended support team up to date with a high-level overview of your sales endeavours and successes is rewarding for them in support of their self-esteem, pride in their contribution and in the company.

NOTES:

93. I plan my next day before I finish for the day

Successful salespeople know that the essence of success is developing, then living the habit of effective planning.

The end of the working day is a great time to take stock of what has been achieved for that day and then to plan the high value activities to be performed the next day.

Of course, there are long term commitments that are made long before the end of the previous day. However, ensuring that before you finish for the day you have a crystal clear view of what you must do the next day allows you to finish work and let your mind focus on what needs to be done rather than being worried that you have missed something.

Remember the '5 P's:
Proper Planning Prevents Poor Performance

Time management is essential. Leaving your planning to the start of the new day wastes a lot of time. I have observed salespeople that arrive at their desk (whether that is remote or their home study) and then start to arrange appointments for the day. By the time they have settled in, sorted through the 'busy tasks' such as e-mails and voice messages, they have already lost an hour. It may take another hour to get an appointment set up or actually get through to talk with their prospect via virtual means.

Contrast this with the sales professional that is well organised and has their following day effectively planned. They will have arranged an appointment and, if it is a remote customer meeting, they can be at that customer's premises by 8:30 the following morning when the less organised salesperson is only just sitting down at their desk.

The other advantage of being prepared by the close of business is that your mind has the opportunity to innovate overnight in preparation for the engagement the next day. Stress levels are lower because you are well prepared and in a calm mental state when you commence your day's activities.

NOTES:

94. The best days to visit customers are bad weather/down time days

Picture this. You are facing some adverse weather or time of year conditions. A voice in your head is telling you: "It's too cold to go out". "It's too wet to go out". "It's too hot go to out". "It's holiday time". "There are no customers available to talk to at this time of year". etc., etc. "Better to spend a day doing the 'stuff in the office' that needs to be done."

Do not listen to that voice in your head. That is what 'ordinary' salespeople do. If you are thinking "No normal salesperson in their right mind would make visits on a day like this" you are right! 'Normal' salespeople wouldn't go out in such conditions – but you are not aiming to be 'normal', you are aiming to be Extraordinary.

It is an ideal time to visit customers when all the other 'normal' salespeople are cosy doing their administration work in prime sales time.

Imagine the great 'warm up' conversations you can have that <u>the client</u> initiates along the lines of "Gee, I'm amazed you would visit on a day like today" and you can say "Calling on customers like you makes it worthwhile going out on a day like this". Corny? Sure. But it will get a laugh and they will secretly admire your tenacity and dedication, putting you ahead of the others that would not think of doing something like that.

Not every customer goes on leave during the 'down times' surrounding summer holidays, festive seasons etc. Making appointments in advance that are in these 'down times' means that you will be talking to your prospective customer whilst others are ignoring them based on the assumption that they are not there.

By all means, if you have taken the necessary activity, made contact with your prospects and customers, then ascertained that there really will not be anyone to call on due to a holiday season, take your holidays at the same time as them rather than saving your leave to take when your customers will be at work (and potentially talking to your competition).

NOTES:

---

95. I spend 80% of my prospecting time qualifying the 20% of prospects that will 'make my target'

It is not how much time you spend prospecting that is important but how well you use that time. Prospecting for leads and opportunities is essential to bring potential customers into the 'funnel' that will lead to sales revenue.

The Pareto Principle applies to the time you spend prospecting. If you set clear criteria for the prospective customers that you know will buy your offering and then only spend your time focused on prospecting with then, it is far more effective than spending the same amount of time with each potential customer.

For example, if you are selling work wear with safety aspects to it, you are better off spending time with industrial and trade suppliers than retail menswear shops. Sure, the odd menswear shop may carry a range of work wear, but this will fall into the '20%' of your sales revenue and could end up consuming 80% of your time educating them, closing the business and coaching them once they agree to stock your product.

Similarly, with services. If you are selling training services, it is best to spend time with organisations that have numerous people that require your offering than smaller organisations that will only have one or two people needing the service. This may sound obvious but it is amazing how many salespeople waste a lot of time convincing a prospect to make a relatively small sale.

There is a saying: "Small fish are sweet". I have found that in sales and business in general, that this is not the case. Small sales absorb a disproportionately large amount of time. Often a small sale will consume as much time and energy as a sale with a transaction value 10 times the size of the small transaction. It is best to think big, pursue the big opportunities and leave the small sales to others, unless of course they are to assist one of your major prospects or large existing customers.

NOTES:

96. I use sales systems to their fullest and assist others with them where I can

Most organisations have electronic systems to support the sales effort. These may have various names such as CRM (Customer Relationship Management) or ERP (Enterprise Resource Planning) or various other acronyms. There are many vendors of these systems including Salesforce.com, Microsoft, Oracle, Zoho, et al.

These systems provide a rich source of information on customers and the transactions that the organisation is either proposing or has done with them.

The high achieving salesperson embraces these systems and looks for ways to take advantage of them to increase their sales effectiveness.

The CRM system will save the salesperson a great deal of time and effort by storing all of the customer details in one central system. It is not unusual for salespeople to be asked to provide lists of customers for particular outbound promotions and other marketing activity. Provided that the information in the system is up to date, the salesperson has the required information at hand and can generate the required list from the system, which in turn means that the requested information is available to the marketing team for their ongoing reference.

It may be that the CRM is integrated with the company's ERP system so that there is a full view of all sales, marketing and commercial activity of the customer. This is an invaluable source of information to enable the sales effort to be targeted to the customer and enable a deeper, more valuable relationship with clients which is mutually beneficial for the client and the salesperson/company.

There are those who have difficulty with these systems. The sales professional is ready to assist others by demonstrating how they are using the systems successfully and recommending ways that less proficient team members can use them.

Naturally the successful salesperson does not lose focus on their own sales activity, but being a 'go to' person for some experienced input for others is a great way for the professional to improve their ability to use the system and hence discover even more effective ways to use the systems to their advantage.

NOTES:

97. I take time out to think before I act, then act decisively

Action is the essence of success provided it is well considered and that it fits into the overall strategy for success.

As you will observe with top ranked tennis players, they don't 'just hit the ball'. They are considered about where they hit it so that they can be prepared for where the opponent will hit the ball in return. They have thought about the placement of the ball prior to hitting it – then they hit it decisively, even if it is a very gentle 'lob'. Because of their training and experience, they are able to position themselves so that they have time to 'think', with those thoughts happening in an instant. It is not a lengthy planning session. Their placement is decided in fractions of a second taking into account the best information they can glean from their opponent's position at the time, their experience and the 'state of play'.

Selling is very similar. It is a highly active arena where unplanned events happen regularly that impact the sales process. The distinction between the average salesperson and the high achiever is that they always take the time required to think through the next action and its consequences rather than simply reacting.

Think of selling as a game of chess. In the advance of the competitor, you can simply react and win the immediate skirmish or you can think through the next moves and thwart their strategy or better still, change the competition to your advantage by executing your longer play strategy.

The sales process is fluid with any number of outcomes possible at every stage. The expert salesperson continually assesses the situations, considers the possible outcomes, including the competitive actions/reactions, then tunes their approach to deal with the current events and set the scene for how they want the process to unfold. Once they have decided on their action, they execute immediately before things change. They are well aware of the strategic advantage that the element of surprise can provide when they are engaged in a highly competitive sales campaign.

Remember, the best way to hit a target is not "shoot, ready, aim" it is a well-planned "Ready, Aim, Fire"!

NOTES:

98. I diligently communicate with my customers and my support team

When you boil it all down, selling is a transaction between two parties: purchaser and vendor. Ideally the transaction is one where each party gains value. Customers buy for their own reasons that will be based upon one, or a combination of, their perceived needs ranging from the basics (e.g. hunger, breathing) through to self-esteem and achieving their full potential as a person (e.g. climbing Mt. Everest).

Average salespeople view the interaction with their customers as a transaction and then move on. The high achieving salespeople take a different approach whereby they collaborate with their customer to address the customer's specific requirement. Rather than it being an 'us and them' approach, the professional works with the prospect so that the customer and the sales professional are collaborating to address the requirement. The customer and the sales professional see themselves as 'on the same side' of the initiative to solve the requirement, not on opposing sides as is the case with the traditional defensive approach of 'salesperson versus prospect' to win a sale.

The basis of this collaboration is diligent communication by the sales professional with the customer and the greater sales team/organisation.

True communication goes both ways. Average salespeople talk a lot but seldom listen, or worse, fail to take the time to properly understand what is being conveyed to them. The high achieving sales professionals listen intently. They, ask questions where necessary to ensure that they are really hearing what their customers want. They continually communicate so that their support teams understand what is required and that their message is being properly interpreted so that the required customer outcome will be achieved.

The sales professional takes the role of advocate for both their company to the customer and concurrently for the customer to the sales support team and into the company. To be an effective advocate, diligent, continual 'two way' communication with the customer and back into the company is essential.

NOTES:

99. No one succeeded by getting 100% for doing nothing

Anxiety about possibly making mistakes or risk of failure can lead to not doing anything. In sales doing nothing is certain to lead to failure.

Sales is very similar to pioneering where you are continually 'in unfamiliar territory'. It involves seeking new customers that have not used the offering before; introducing new offerings to customers who are not familiar with them and often introducing new, innovative offerings that are fresh out of research and development. A truism is "pioneers end up with wounds from the bears..." however if the pioneers were not prepared to pioneer new territory, make mistakes and overcome the adversities, there would be no progress.

The successful salesperson pre-prepares as far as possible in the limited time frame and then DOES SOMETHING. First presentations that are made often fall flat due to unforeseen questions that cannot be answered, because they are pitched at the wrong level or to the wrong potential customer. Based on the experience, the salesperson that has made that presentation can then reassess what happened; what went right, what didn't work and then tailor their approach to DO IT AGAIN.

The salesperson that procrastinates and doesn't make presentations/approaches until they have perfected them will often be too late, having lost the opportunity in favour of another more active salesperson that presented, made mistakes and then worked with the customer to address any issues out of the first approach.

No child learns to walk without first stumbling, falling and then getting up again. With each attempt they gain confidence, learn from their mistake and finally master walking. Sales is no different. Overcoming the 'fear of failure' or 'looking silly' is a constant struggle but one that the successful salesperson deals with regularly and conquers.

The arch enemy of successful sales is doing nothing. Be prepared to be rejected – there is always the next prospect. Be prepared to make errors in your pitch – it may lead to uncovering an unidentified need/selling point that will clinch the deal. Be prepared to have a sale fall through because there was an error in the specification – how you deal with it may mean that you gain a long-term customer based on their respect of your integrity and ability to deal with adversity. There is only one mistake that you should be terrified of and that is the mistake of doing nothing.

NOTES:

100. I get the best facts available then act decisively

We have all done it. Information comes to our attention, we ask a few questions of people that may or may not know the reality then formulate an opinion after which we take action – only to find out that the situation was not as it seemed and we look foolish at best or lose the business or damage our credibility at worst.

Decisive action should only be taken after appropriate effort has been taken to get as may facts as possible in the time available, not circumstantial evidence, hearsay or a perceived reality.

I was made aware of a situation where a presentation was made to a potential customer for a mulita million-dollar sale of communication equipment that included all the reasons why the customer should not consider a competitor's offering. The inclusions of the reasons for not purchasing the competitor's product was based on the assumption that the competitor was being considered. During the presentation the CEO of the customer stopped the presentation and asked his deputy "Why haven't we had a presentation by that competitor?" When told they weren't being considered his response was "Well if this company presenting sees them as so important that they have to tell us why we shouldn't consider them then I want to hear from them!" They requested a presentation from the competitor who went on to win the business and become a leader in that market. If only the salesperson had got the facts and knew that the competitor they highlighted was not being considered, they may have won the deal.

Worrying unduly about unfounded matters along the lines of 'what might be' or 'what if this goes wrong' or 'I hear the customer is not going to consider us' is futile, drains energy and can lead to procrastination. Continued effort to get as many facts as possible will lead to deeper conversations with the customer which will in turn lead to the ability to take decisive action to win business. Where negative information is uncovered it can be dealt with appropriately and decisively. Even if this means 'walking away from the business' it is better to qualify the situation early and move on to a more lucrative pursuit that better utilized the valuable commodity of your time.

NOTES:

---

101. My plans are useless unless I put them into action

Everyone knows that if you want to achieve something you need a plan. When asked "Do you have a plan on how you will achieve your targets/goals?" many salespeople respond "Definitely!" When the conversation moves on with the question "Great, so is it in writing and can we go through your written plan?" many of the salespeople will not have the plan in writing and only be able to give a vague explanation as to how they will achieve their goals. In reality, they don't have a well-defined goal and in many cases these 'goals' are dreams.

Of the salespeople that do have a written plan, very few of them will be able to demonstrate how they will put their plan into action and measure their outcomes. This is called 'execution' and it is not well understood by the majority of salespeople.

You would not attempt to build a house without a plan and if you are paying a contractor to build it you expect to see clear progress with detailed documentation surrounding the expenditure of your funds, compliance with regulations etc. It is the same for your plan to achieve your targets/goals.

The plan must have a clearly defined set of actions with outcomes defined against each of them that will be achieved within a specific time. Use the S-M-A-R-T principle for goals/targets: Specific, Measurable, Achievable, Realistic and Time-based.

Keep the list of actions, the specific outcomes that will be achieved and the date/time by which they will be achieved in your folder and review them at least weekly or better still, daily. Update the list with your progress so that you can track your progress toward achieving the goal/target. If necessary, break the goal/target down into smaller actions and work to systematically achieve those until the larger goal is met.

This process will mean that you can track your progress and where necessary adjust the actions that you are taking. You may find that some actions become irrelevant and new ones are required. It's your list to adjust as necessary but make sure that you are making progress as a result of your actions. It's not about being busy, it's about being effective. Remember, a goal without a plan is a dream and a plan without action that is tracked is a wish list. Dreams and wishes don't make money – outcomes that satisfy customers do.

NOTES

Section 5

Last but not least

102. Closing Secret: ENJOY!!

Life is not all about being successful in your profession. Sure, being successful in your vocation is important if you are to support your lifestyle, however if you don't take the time to enjoy the fruits of your labours, what is the point?

If you want to cut down a big tree, you better make sure that you sharpen the axe first and then take time out to hone it from time to time to ensure that it is sharp or you will have to work continually harder as the axe gets blunt from work. You are like that axe.

Continually pushing yourself without taking regular time out for enjoyment, whether with your family, friends or on your own, is counterproductive. Athletes have found that a critical part of training for endurance sports is scheduling rest into their regimens or they run the risk of injury or breaking down. Being a successful salesperson is very similar to being an endurance athlete in that respect.

There will be times where a sustained effort is required over a relatively long period. These times can be stimulating, particularly when they lead to a positive outcome. No matter how intense and extended the effort is, with appropriate planning time can always be found for enjoyment even if it is for short periods.

Time spent enjoying something entirely different from work 'recharges your batteries'. Often problems that were seemingly insurmountable before taking a break take on a new perspective and are easily addressed once you have enjoyed some relaxation or an activity that 'takes your mind off work'.

Enjoyment will take whatever form suits you and your desires. Some will do extreme pursuits like mountain climbing, mountain bike riding, long distance running or sky diving. Others will relax with family and friends or take relaxed strolls in the country or on the beach. It may be tinkering with old cars or playing a musical instrument. Many of the highly successful people do a combination of several of these and have a hobby that they enjoy to relax and reinvigorate themselves.

By being successful at sales, you are not only fulfilling your mission but providing income for others who rely on you to make sales. Make sure you take the time you deserve to gain the benefit from your efforts and ENJOY!

NOTES:

Bibliography

1. **Maslow.** Maslow's hierarchy of needs. *Wikipedia.* [Online] 2019. https://en.wikipedia.org/wiki/Maslow's_hierarchy_of_needs.

2. **McKoll-Kennedy, Kreil, Lusch, Lusch.** Marketing Concepts and Strategies. *Marketing Concepts and Strategies.* Belmont : Thomas Nelson, 1992, pp. 111,112.

3. **Tzu, Sun.** *The Art of War (Edited and with a forward by James Clavell).* New York : Dell Publishing, 1983

Recommended Reading

The Art of War	Sun Tzu
How to Master the Art of Selling	Tom Hopkins
Spin Selling	Neil Rackham
The 7 Habits of Highly Effective People	Stephen Covey
Think and Grow Rich	Napoleon Hil
Success Through a Positive Mental Attitude	W. Clement Stone
The Richest Man in Babylon	George S. Clason
Power Base Selling	Jim Holden
Trout on Strategy	Jack Trout
Marketing Insights From A to Z	Philip Kotler
Getting It Done	Roger Fisher & Alan Sharp
No Bull Selling	Hank Trisler
Lateral Thinking	Edward De Bono
Getting to Yes	Fisher & William Ury
Who Moved My Cheese?	Dr Spencer Johnson

ABOUT THE AUTHOR

Philip Belcher is CEO of SalesAbility and Managing Director of its parent company, LSE Consulting Pty Ltd, a management consulting company focused on, business growth, turn around and exit readiness.

SalesAbility was founded to enable superior sales performance through providing sales education, consulting, resources and systems

He has over 30 years of success in sales, sales management and management/leadership of high technology companies, as an entrepreneur and management consultant. Throughout his career, he has been responsible for sales in excess of $2bn dollars in industries including high technology, real estate and fast foods.

Philip has held CEO, Managing Director, Executive Director, Non-executive Director, GM, Senior Sales and technical positions with high profile companies including Cisco Systems, StorageTek (now Oracle), Datacraft Australia, Datacraft Ltd, Dimension Data, NEC, AWA Ltd, Fairlight.AU, Radware, PM-Partners group and Telecom Australia.

His specialisation is sales enablement, strategy definition/execution; business turn-around, re-engineering and change leadership. He has experience in Australia, New Zealand, Asia, South East Asia and the Pacific.

Philip was a Board member of Box Hill Institute of TAFE, Victoria for 12 years during which period he held the position of Joint Deputy Chairperson and has held the positions of Vice President Australia and President of the NSW Branch of the Institute of Management Consultants.

Philip holds an MBA from the Macquarie University Graduate School of Management, is a Fellow of the Australian Institute of Company Directors, a Fellow of the Institute of Managers and Leaders (previously Australian Institute of Managers) and achieved the status of Certified Management Consultant with the Institute of Management Consultants.

www.ingramcontent.com/pod-product-compliance
Lightning Source LLC
Chambersburg PA
CBHW071622170426
43195CB00038B/1855